THE SELFISH GUIDE

THE SELFISH GUIDE TO FULFILLMENT, MEANING, AND PURPOSE

CARLOS VILLAFUERTE

ISBN 979-8-9892994-1-6

First edition October 2023
Writer by Carlos Villafuerte
Edited by Rachel Small
Cover & Design by Kiryl Lysenka
Published by Cultum Vita LLC
www.CultumVita.com

Disclaimer

While all the stories in this book are based on actual events, names and specific details have been changed, both to protect the privacy of the people involved and for ease of reading. Also, some events have been compressed, and some dialogue has been recreated. The book reflects the author's present recollections of past experiences.

Acknowledgment

Thank-you God. A profound thank-you to Juliet Braslow, my wife, for always supporting me. My life is better every day because you are in it. A heartfelt thank-you to Rodolfo Castro, my grandfather, for taking so much time to nurture my mind as I was growing up. A loving thank-you to Carmen and Robert Villafuerte, my mother, and father, for raising me to become who I am today. A special thank-you to Rachel Small, my editor, for guiding me and my writing. Lastly, thank-you to the family and friends who have supported me on this journey, One Voice Scholars, Quest Leadership (now QuestBridge), and Philip Evans Scholars.

Table of Content

AN APPETIZER TO SPARK CURIOSITY

You need to be selfish to be able to live a life of fulfillment, meaning, and purpose. You might be thinking, "But, Carlos, being selfish goes against everything I've been taught!"

When I talk about being selfish, I'm not saying eat all the food at the table and leave none for others. I'm saying eat what you need to feel full. If you're hungry, how are you going to help others or enjoy your time with them? Fullness—self-satisfaction—is a worthy goal. The difficulty lies in knowing when you're full. In a world of excess and noise, we're not taught to recognize self-satisfaction in the moment.

This book will help you learn to do that. It will help you learn to recognize fullness and take care of yourself first. And I love to cook, so get ready for a lot of food analogies!

Who I am

I've always been, well, different. From a very young age, I wanted to know "the answer" to life. After asking a million questions I discovered there is no one correct answer—because what's best for one person is usually only best for them.

So, I changed course and began seeking out wisdom. I wanted the knowledge to be able to decide what was best for me. After reading a lot of books, mostly by dead old white guys, I discovered that this would be hard—likely the hardest thing I'd ever done.

Once again, I changed my approach. I started chasing so-called universal truths. I kept a notebook handy and wrote in it whenever I encountered something with a speck of universal wisdom. I wanted to go back to basics, to start from the bottom, and build something that could guide me. Over time, I discovered that despite being true, many universal truths often didn't apply to me, and unbeknownst to me, that is when I started to write this guide. I was nine.

I struggled as a kid. As a minority kid living in Los Angeles, I grew up in an environment that was machismo, strict, religious, and abusive. All I wanted was a fighting chance. I knew the odds were against me, but the thought of fighting to the mountaintop only to look around and realize I was on the wrong mountain was overwhelming. I wanted someone or something to guide me to the right mountain. I didn't want an answer simply handed to me—I'd already learned that things given were seldom appreciated. I just wanted a guide to give me some direction, to help me get started. I read a lot, I talked to my elders, and at every opportunity, I asked questions and pursued answers, hoping to find patterns.

I came to discover that the key to getting up the mountain was simply trying a new thing, consistently and consciously.

When I tried new things I was able to rise above the noise and trust myself. Then I started helping others do the same, as a coach and speaker. Helping people gives me purpose. That's why I wrote this guide—to offer others a bridge to fulfillment, meaning, and purpose.

What this book is, and what it's not

This book is not a step-by-step guide to finding "the answers." Instead, it's a framework to help you create a system that works for *you*—a system of tools, skills, and habits to help you embrace who you are. The specific path you take right now doesn't matter. What matters is becoming conscious of how you're living your life and taking control where you can so you're living in a way that's true to you.

What matters is trying things and being present as you do.

This book will offer guidance to help you determine where you're heading and how to adjust your course, if that's what you desire, through a framework that addresses *who you are*. Finding your answers, the ones specific to you, is about consistently adjusting your system over time.

We hear it often: "Life is a journey. It's about the process, not the result." The way is fulfilling in itself. It's with this in mind that I wrote this guide.

The guidance in this book will give you the tools to cultivate your garden, but you need to do the planting and be consistent in how you care for it over time. You need to choose what you plant in it.

And the best time to start is now. You are enough now.

How this book is structured

The Selfish Guide to Fulfillment, Meaning, and Purpose is comprised of three parts: *Breakfast*, *Lunch*, and *Dinner* (yes, I like food analogies!). This structure reflects my training program and my coaching program. You don't need to complete each part before moving to the next, but it will be easier if you do, as they build on each other. Each is designed to help you understand yourself better.

When I first start working with a client, I like to determine what's taking up most of their energy and then work through the parts of my program with them that focus on those issues. You might try doing the same as you read this book. Before getting into the parts, consider what you're thinking about the most and what might be beneficial for you to address.

Each part is filled with relatable stories, practical advice, and easy-to-implement strategies to help you cultivate a life of fulfillment, meaning, and purpose. Each chapter starts with a story to illustrate an idea that is the focus of that chapter. The main idea of the chapter is then broken down into practical bites. The end of each chapter has an example of a reflection session, as well as takeaways and questions you can use for your own reflection sessions.

A note about the use of *short term*, *medium term*, and *long term*

Throughout this guide, short term will refer to now, the next hour, or today. The short term tends to be the urgent, your how, involves your emotions, perception, or something the world wants of you. The medium term refers to tomorrow, next week, or next month. The medium term tends to involve urgent and important, your why or what others want of you. The long term refers to months, years, or even decades. The long term tends to involve direction, the important, habits or something for you.

The short-term goal of this guide is to help you understand yourself, others, and what you do. The medium-term goal is to help you accept yourself, others, and what you do. The long-term goal is to help you embrace yourself, others, and what you do. As we'll explore, it's important to take all three into account—the short, medium, and long term—as you go through life.

Start with you

You need to get to know yourself before you start thinking about others or the world. Remember, everyone wins when you put yourself first. Unfortunately, everything that isn't you tends to cloud your inner vision and make it challenging to understand yourself. You need to practice blocking out the noise with the right tools so you can hear and trust your voice. In turn, you can accept and embrace yourself. Often, this means being selfish.

The idea of putting yourself first isn't new, but it's easier said than done. The concepts in this guide are simple but challenging. Start small and be consistent. Know that you can do this.

I considered many approaches before writing this guide. At first, I planned to use examples featuring well-known individuals, but ultimately, through adjusting my own system over time, I determined that since I communicate and connect most effectively through telling personal stories, it would be best to write my book with that as my compass.

My hope is that my stories and my experiences, will help you. I hope that this guide will empower you to put yourself first so you can be present with yourself and then with others and your life. I hope that this guide will help you keep moving forward consistently, even if only in the smallest increments.

This is the guide I wish I had as a kid.

* * *

PART ONE
BREAKFAST WITH THE SOUL: FULFILLMENT

"Breakfast," which is made up of Chapters One to Three, focuses on a set of powerful tools to help you unlock the potential of reflection. Breakfast is all about understanding, accepting, and ultimately embracing who you are, so you can learn to love yourself unconditionally. By doing so, you'll lay a solid foundation for fulfillment.

Fulfillment is that feeling of self-satisfaction that comes from living life on your terms—from living in a way that feels authentic and true to who you are. It's about creating a sense of belonging within yourself, so you can be fully present in the moment and enjoy every aspect of your life.

Breakfast will teach you to tap into a deep sense of self-awareness. With this self-awareness, you can live a life that resonates with you. You'll learn to embrace your uniqueness and create a path to fulfillment that will allow you to be in the moment—now.

CHAPTER ONE

REFLECTION

Reflection is processing life, it gives sight.

Focus: In this chapter, we'll explore the importance of reflection and how to get started with it. Reflection looks different for everyone, but the trick is to get into the habit of doing it every day. Start with just two minutes of reflection each day and build on this gradually. It's all about being consistent—and starting now.

Story

I'm driving and struggling to stay awake.

"Stay awake, stay awake, stay awake!" I say aloud.

Did I fall asleep at the light? No. Well, *maybe . . .*

I've slept only a couple of hours the past week. I feel as if my body is experiencing slow Internet. My sense of reality is fuzzy; everything feels distant. All I want is to curl up in a ball and cry, but I must focus and get to the hospital.

Little bits of time, like seconds at a stoplight, feel like an eternity. I feel empty. I feel lost and alone. I have to keep going, no matter what.

* * *

It was the darkest and coldest point of my life, so it's hard to believe that just a week earlier, I'd experienced one of the most wonderful moments of my life. My wife and I were about to have friends over when her water broke. Five weeks early, but that wasn't unheard of. We didn't panic. We had a bag ready, and we even had copies of the birth plan written down and ready to hand out. We were prepared, knew what we wanted, and had done everything to ensure the plan would work, or at least have the best odds of it working.

Really, we were grasping for control. We had no idea what we were doing–it was our first child, and we were in a foreign country. But we'd seen the results of planning and hard work in our lives, so we'd grounded ourselves in what was most likely to happen and prepared accordingly.

The reality was soon to be unfathomable.

On the way to the hospital, I was nervously excited. *I might be a father tonight!* We were taken to a room immediately. The nurse checked my wife and said the doctor would be in shortly. As we waited in that small, cold consultation room, I felt as if blood were refusing to circulate to my extremities. My hands were freezing, and I was so anxious, but I kept calm for my wife. How long was "shortly"? One minute? Five? Twenty?

It seemed we waited forever, but the doctor checked on my wife within a few minutes. Calm and matter-of-fact, he said she was far along. He asked us when her water broke, and when we told him, he made a strange face.

What did that mean?

"It's fine," he said. "Just very fast. We'll move you to a room now, no need to worry."

That's when I started to truly worry.

On the walk to our room, my mind raced. *What should I be doing right now?* I wanted to be useful but was uncertain what to do and didn't feel my wife would appreciate the twenty questions going through my head. Understandably, she seemed preoccupied with the prospect of life coming out of her shortly. The path became clear: my mission was to ensure my wife got everything requested in our birth plan.

In the room, we were pleasantly surprised to find our midwife. She seemed calm, but I was still on a mission. I turned off the lights.

I started the playlist I'd spent days making. I set up the yoga ball and asked my wife if she wanted to try it. She swayed back and forth, clearly in a lot of pain, and didn't seem convinced it would help, but she came over anyway. I gave her a massage, tried some pressure points, and coached her on her breathing.

Earlier, we'd created a chant of words and sounds, and I started repeating them to her. It was beautiful. Time stood still. I focused on her and was in that moment with her. It was just us. I forgot about all the unknowns and uncertainty. Being there, in the present moment, allowed me to overcome my worry.

A couple of hours after my wife's water broke, it was time. The midwife directed her into a squatting position, and our baby was born in a matter of minutes.

In seconds, the room was filled with a dozen people. I was overwhelmed. What was happening? What should I be doing? I was handed a pair of scissors and asked if I wanted to cut the cord. Instinctually, I said yes. Then I was given the baby, and once again time stood still. Love at first sight. An avalanche of joy. I hadn't known it was possible to feel such a strong bond so quickly. It was glorious. I felt as if I'd been holding my breath for hours and now could not only breathe but breathe the most incredible air. Holding our baby felt like a miracle. I was the luckiest person in the world.

A staff member took the baby, and after doing some measurements and tests, they gave them (gender neutral terminology) back to my wife and me and assured us everything was normal. Our relief deepened. My wife held our baby and I held her and nothing could be better than this, this moment.

We were taken to a different room, where my wife was asked to attempt to breastfeed. She tried without success, but I wasn't worried. We knew it could be difficult. We requested a breastfeeding nurse to assist us. Next, we video-called our families. The conversations were sweet and a bit distant, but we'd expected as much, being so far away.

What exactly happened next is still a blur.

The breastfeeding nurse arrived and attempted to help, but we still had no luck. And then we were told the baby needed to be taken urgently, as it was concerning that they hadn't eaten since birth. My wife and I were taken aback but we told ourselves everything would be okay. At this point, it was past midnight, so we tried to sleep.

An hour later, I stood up from the pull-out sofa to check on my wife. She was wide awake, just as I was. Something was wrong. I could feel it. I couldn't shake the sinking feeling in the pit of my stomach.

The nurse hadn't been clear on how long the baby would be gone. Thoughts of second-guessing circled in my head. *We should have tried harder to feed them. We shouldn't have called our families and wasted that time. Should we have known how critical the situation was? Am I a bad parent already?*

We called the nurses' station and were told we'd be updated when they had an update. The uncertainty grew until it became sickening.

My wife and I didn't sleep that night and, despite what we'd been told, called for an update every few hours. We didn't get one. The agony of this limbo was soul crushing. The connection with my baby was so strong that every second away from them felt like a gash in my flesh. Could I be doing anything to help? Would anything I came up with be feasible in this country?

Finally, after ten hours, staff informed us that our baby still wasn't eating and had been taken to the ICU. We'd be notified when I could visit. My wife would have to wait, as the hospital had a strict policy: twenty-four hours of bed rest for patients who'd just given birth. Again, the information was unclear. How long would I have to wait? Throughout the morning I went to the front desk multiple times and always got the same response: things were uncertain and we'd get a call when possible. I eventually learned that our baby still wasn't suckling. They were refusing formula.

Don't panic, I repeated to myself. *Be a good husband and father. Stay focused.*

Our baby needed a tube in their stomach because they weren't eating. They needed oxygen because they didn't have enough in their blood. They needed to be in a temperature-regulated box because they couldn't regulate their temperature. And the most concerning—they had hypotonia. Their body was limp and unresponsive to stimuli. I asked what this meant, precisely.

"They don't cry," the nurse said. "Ever."

It was like a punch to the gut. Everyone knew babies and crying went together. With that news I fell into an abyss of despair. Each of these issues alone was concerning, but together they were in a different realm of horror. *Why? What do we do? How do I tell my wife?*

When I finally saw my baby, I struggled to stand. So close yet so far from me, in a tiny box all alone. I didn't know it was possible to feel so much pain for another human being. I would have done anything to trade places with them. They looked so helpless; I felt so powerless. I was supposed to be able to care for my baby. Instead, I could do nothing but watch.

So began weeks of torture. I struggled to exist. Every few days a new specialist was brought in, a new test was done. Maybe it was a rare genetic disorder? Maybe it was one of a dozen other things, all bad? The outcome was always the same, inconclusive, and the staff members' expressions always suggested that tomorrow probably wouldn't come for our baby.

Then, to add insult to injury, our baby developed a heart problem—their brain was forgetting to tell their heart to beat. *What? How? Why?* Meanwhile, we learned that my wife had broken her sacrum in labor.

We were told that the best thing we could do for our baby was for my wife to provide breast milk to feed our baby via a gastric feeding tube and spend as much time with them as we could. So that's what we did. We sacrificed sleep and feeding ourselves to spend every possible second with them. My wife and I were in the worst mental and physical states possible. We could think of only one thing: we had to be with our baby, no matter what.

With every moment we spent with them, our love grew. And as my love grew, so did my fear of losing them. I feared I might not recover from such a loss. I was loving someone more than I'd ever loved anyone while knowing there was a good chance that they'd stop breathing at any moment.

I had no control over what would happen next. I had control only over what I did in the moment, so I focused on that. I didn't think of what was next, only what was now. I was fully present when I was with my baby, but when I wasn't with them, I went to the darkest, scariest place in my mind. The dread of the unknown grew daily, consuming the little left of me.

After the first week, I knew something had to change. I had no energy left. I told my wife we couldn't continue like this. We needed to take care of ourselves first. When in doubt, do.

I kept breaking down numerous times a day, but after every episode, I started asking myself, *What do you need?* The answer was always clear: *I need to think long term.* That meant taking care of myself now so I could keep going, however far I needed to go. This moment of reflection, this simple act of asking myself what I needed, allowed me to acknowledge my pain and my situation.

What did I need? I needed to be present for my baby. How could I do this? I needed to process my emotions rather than ignore them. That meant acknowledging, accepting, and then embracing—feeling—them, so I could let them go. I needed to deal with the pain. I was maxed out. To continue, I had to process and unload.

Of course, I had little energy to process my emotions, but I knew that doing so was necessary to stay grounded in reality. So my wife and I made a plan to process what we were going through. This plan involved making sure we slept for six hours every night. It involved acknowledging and talking about what we were feeling. The drive to the hospital was always hard—would we arrive to find a lifeless baby?—so we played cheerful music on the way. (To this day, there are certain songs that stop me in my tracks. I'll get a lump in my throat, and the hairs on my arms will rise.) We scheduled a time to speak to a professional. We made sure to eat. Ultimately, we chose not to visit the NICU during one visitation window—the one with the most traffic. This gave us time to meet our sleeping and eating requirements. I also allowed myself to continue breaking down when I needed to.

The torture continued to intensify, but scheduling time to process it made all the difference. It allowed me to recognize the real problem: I needed to feel the fear. I'd been trying to skip the feeling part. I'd wanted to jump to the solution. There's no substitute for simply acknowledging and allowing yourself to feel what you're feeling. I needed to trust that I could handle it. At one point, I let go and cried myself to exhaustion in a ball in the shower. Allowing myself to feel the fear didn't end up overwhelming me, as I'd expected it to. Instead, it helped me get to a place where I could genuinely accept my situation, which helped me hang on.

The only thing my wife and I could do for our baby was spend time with them, but we also needed to think long term and to persevere. If we didn't care for ourselves, how could we help our baby?

Whenever we thought we couldn't hang on anymore we focused on the present moment and kept hanging on. Every day I reached a new personal limit.

I found the strength to cherish every moment. To cherish the present. Despite the growing difficulties, my wife and I had faith that we could grow to meet them because we understood and accepted ourselves as we were in the moment.

Breaking it down

Part One, Breakfast, is all about you. Not you in the world or you with other people, but the true you. The you within. The work in this part is designed to help you acknowledge yourself, as you are now, through reflection. This may sound simple in theory, but it's challenging in practice.

To understand yourself you need to be able to hear your voice through all the noise—the media, family, friends, work, and everything else. This is difficult. Many people are scared that they won't like the person underneath the noise. But you have to start somewhere. Avoiding yourself won't make you go away. Start with reflection.

Reflection allows you to see yourself from a holistic perspective. The more you reflect, the more you start to view yourself as a puzzle—you become more apparent to yourself as you put together the pieces over time. It takes practice. As you'll encounter in the stories throughout this guide, it's often those difficult times that breed growth and perspective. In those times you must be willing to listen to yourself.

Reflection is a key part of building a system that works for you. It's vital to give yourself time to reflect on what's happening in your head.

So how do you reflect, exactly?

Reflection is simply processing what's going on in your life and in your mind. You'll need to set aside time to do this. If you think you have no time, make time. Start with just two minutes, although five is better, perhaps at the beginning or the end of your day, until it becomes a habit. You'll likely spend more and more time reflecting the longer you continue this practice. The secret is that you always have time—you must intentionally give up something less important. Just as you need to eat and sleep to keep your body healthy, you need to reflect to keep your mind healthy.

We are emotional beings, whether we like it or not, so I suggest starting there: by reflecting on your emotions.

Here are a few questions you might start with:

- What's the strongest emotion I felt today?
- What am I thinking and/or feeling, and why?
- Why, why, why, why, why? (When in doubt, ask questions like a toddler.)

Keep some paper and a pen handy so you can write down what comes to you. At this point, you don't need to process whatever comes up. Simply set a time to do so in the future. Maybe you schedule it in your day planner, put it on your to-do list, or set a deadline for processing it. What's important is that you do process it at some point. Otherwise, it will keep coming back, louder and louder. Try to not compare yourself to others, instead compare yourself to your past self.

To clarify, when I talk about processing, I'm referring to doing what you need in order to let go. Processing can be mental, like acknowledging, accepting, or embracing through reflection. Processing can be physical, like screaming, crying, running, dancing or exercise. Often it is both mental and physical like singing, dancing, cooking, art, or games. The way you know you have processed an emotion is when you stop taking it personally, when you stop judging, or when it simply stops influencing you. In short, you can take a step back and look at your situation from a third person perspective without getting emotional. The pain will still be there, but it stops clouding your perspective. Letting go allows you to learn and grow. Addressing and processing are the same things. Processing tends to take more time and energy.

Don't fight what comes up. Write it down. Strive to reflect as an observer, as a person seeing your life from a big-picture perspective without bias. It will be normal to have many random thoughts. If you keep returning to the same ones, write them down, create a plan to process them, and then do it.

I suggest ending your reflection time with a simple practice of gratitude. Reflection can be challenging, ending with gratitude can leave you feeling better. At the end of a reflection session I generally ask clients to list two or three things they're grateful for. By getting in the habit of ending your daily reflection time this way, you'll secure a sense of self-satisfaction. In my experience, it's the most effective way to motivate yourself to keep coming back to the practice, which is crucial.

If you're still struggling with what to reflect on, reflect on death. It will help you appreciate the present and what's most important to you.

Digging deeper into emotions

Know that feelings aren't good or bad–they're simply information. The moment you feel them, they're valid. End of discussion. Process them as best as you can, and then let them go. You can process emotions in numerous ways. Processing might involve crying, running, screaming, hugging, smiling, or other sorts of physical actions. It can involve venting to a trusted person. It can be mental–maybe you curse out a person in your head or think about the worst-case scenario. *What's important is allowing the emotion to take control for a while, so you get to the point where the emotion stops controlling you.*

Sometimes simply reducing the intensity of the emotion is enough. Sometimes you need to continue processing until the emotion dissipates completely. From here, you can learn and grow.

Emotions are huge obstacles for so many of us. In our society, we're generally taught to ignore our emotions or worse–to shove them down deep and deny them. If you're struggling to allow yourself to feel, ask yourself why.

Why? Why? Why?

Keep asking why until a feeling emerges. Then acknowledge its validity. For example, take Karl, a client. He gave a poor presentation at work, and in a session with me, he reflected on it (note that we have an established relationship based on trust and respect).

"How do you feel about how the presentation went?" I asked him.

"I feel nothing," Karl replied.

"Nothing? Why?"

"Because what happened, happened. I screwed up."

"Does it matter that you screwed up?"

"Yes. I wanted to do well."

"Why did you want to do well?"

"I don't want coworkers to think I'm dumb. I hate it when others think that of me."

"Why do you hate it?"

"Because the idea of them thinking less of me angers me."

"Why?"

"Because I care about these people."

"You care about these people? Why?"

"Because they're important to me. I value and respect their opinions."

In our conversation, Karl went from feeling nothing, to feeling angry, to realizing that he felt angry because he valued the people around him. He found and felt his emotion and, in the process, found the motivation to resolve the issue that had led to the poor presentation.

Remember, an emotion isn't positive or negative. "Bad" and "good" feelings go together—you hurt because you care, you hate because you love, you mourn because you valued. It's a two-sided coin: pain on one side and growth on the other.

When you're reflecting on your emotions, stick to the facts as much as possible. Be a detective and let curiosity guide you. Ask yourself what, why, and how. During my time in the hospital with my child, I kept asking these questions over the course of several reflection sessions until I found my fear.

- What is it that I'm feeling? (Attempt to label it—it helps.)
- Why am I feeling this way? (What does the emotion stem from?)
- How do I process this feeling?

I like to think of emotions in terms of a pressure cooker. Your body and mind are the pot, trying to communicate with you. Something in life is applying heat, causing pressure—your emotions. This pressure is neither good nor bad. You can take the pot away from the heat and slowly let the pressure dissipate. Or you can release the valve and let it all rush out. Either way, you must release the pressure. You must release your emotions before you can look inside and grow.

Your body is always trying to tell you something. Stop and listen. It's so easy to get caught up in the world, in the past or the future. Reflecting on and processing your emotions allows you to get back into your life, at this very moment. Set aside time to do this. Maybe set a timer. When the time is up, do your best to let the emotion go. If you cannot, set a time in the future to return to it. Rinse and repeat until you can let it go.

Reflection in action

Jules, a client, was passed up for a promotion. Here's how he reflected on the situation and processed his emotions.

What exactly happened?

The committee said I was great but not good enough because of my performance review. This upset me.

Why did it upset me?

Because I work so hard.

Why do you work so hard?

At this point, he started cursing and screaming out loud. He was in his car on his way home and couldn't think about this anymore.

I'll think about it when I'm home.

Then he put on one of his favorite playlists and turned up the volume. When he got home, he was still fuming. He put on his running shoes and headed out. He ran until he had nothing left, then he turned around. On the jog back home, he tried to reflect again.

I work hard because I care about the job.

Why?

I care about the people I help.

How do you show this?

I prioritize the client and don't care if I get any credit.

How is this evident?

I help our team reach the best outcomes for our clients, regardless of whose client it is.

Why does upper management not see this?

Because my performance review didn't take this into account. I go where I'm needed. I'm everywhere but nowhere.

How can you make this clear?

Through my coworkers. The committee can talk to them. They've all mentioned how critical I've been.

After this, he felt better.

What should I do now?

I'm going to ask the committee to reconsider. I'll tell them that my performance review isn't an adequate picture of my performance and will request that they talk to my coworkers, so they can get a clearer picture.

Just as I did in the hospital, Jules set aside time to reflect and then allowed himself to feel his emotions. For a while, we both felt worse, but then we felt better.

Once you truly feel your emotions, they stop having power over you. Allowing yourself to feel doesn't mean you're allowing your emotions to control your actions. It means you're embracing your emotions and can use them.

For example, take Keith, another client. In a session, he told me about a difficult reflection session he'd had that week. His coworker had thrown him under the bus. A project had failed to launch due to a missed deadline. When pressed, his coworker told their boss that the project had failed because Keith's team hadn't moved quickly enough.

How do I feel?

Betrayed.

After acknowledging this, he did a boxing workout and felt a little better. Then he continued reflecting.

Why did I feel betrayed?

The real issue was out of my hands. My coworker and I both knew this.

At this point, he wanted to go to their boss and say that if anyone was to blame, it was his coworker. It was his coworker's team's responsibility to bring up potential issues to his team in a timely manner. Keith had been given just one day to do something that usually took a week.

Why don't I just go to my boss and tell him this?

Because that's not fair. My coworker is overworked. His team is a person short.

Why does this matter?

It's not who I am. I don't throw people under the bus.

Why?

I value how I do things. I look at the bigger picture.

Why?

Long term, this is how I feel satisfied in myself.

He felt better at this point.

What should I do?

I'll meet with my coworker to try to understand why he did it. I'll also set up a meeting with our boss to highlight the real issue: my coworker being down a person for months now.

He then set both meetings for the next day.

Instead of letting his emotion control his actions, Keith reflected and processed it. He let himself feel betrayed, and when he felt better, he thought of a resolution. Most importantly, he chose a resolution that allowed him to remain true to himself. In my case, it wasn't until after I let myself feel and break down that I was able to realize what I needed to do to continue.

You might not always have time to do this kind of reflection in the moment. That's okay. Set aside time to do so. Maybe you're in a situation where you can't fully feel a particular emotion in that moment, such as at work. If that is the case, acknowledge it and again, set aside time later to feel it. The first few times, it might feel intense and awkward. Know that it gets easier with practice. And remember that nothing lasts forever. Eventually, the emotion will subside, no matter how intense.

I like to imagine my emotions as a bear that I need to hug as hard as possible. They bite and try to get away, and when I start thinking I can no longer hang on, I continue. They always eventually dissipate.

A *note about reflecting on your emotions*: If you're just getting started with reflecting, I don't recommend focusing on old, pent-up emotions. Start with current emotions. For example, if someone slams the door in your face and you get angry, be angry. Feel it. You don't need to express your anger to the person. Simply feel angry and acknowledge that you're feeling angry. Then accept it—tell yourself that it's okay to feel angry. This kind of acceptance is liberating.

As you get more comfortable with reflecting, dig deeper into the emotions that have been under the surface for a while. Intense emotions don't go away if you don't feel them in the moment. They just get pushed down repeatedly until you cannot push anymore, and eventually they explode out of you in one way or another. Unfortunately, this can end up hurting not just you but those you love the most.

Everyone feels their emotions differently, so do what feels right for you while not hurting others.

Tip for starting your reflection practice

- Start small and pretend you're a reporter asking yourself about what happened during your day. Really listen to yourself answering.
- Give yourself a time limit. Start with five minutes once a day. Ideally when you first wake up. Then try five minutes twice a day, adding before bed. Increase the time little by little. Do this until it feels too much, then cut back a little. The trick is to reflect consistently. Find the sweet spot for you.
- Be kind to yourself and end with gratitude. Think about something you appreciate.
- Focus on what's important to you, not to anyone else.
- Try reflecting on a walk, or in the dark. Try out different environments.
- Make a list of a few things that you could do to help you reflect, then try one different thing on the list every week. (This will help you build a system that works for you—more on this in the 3rd part of the book.) Again, be consistent. The ideas don't have to be perfect, or even good, just different from each other. Keep tweaking until you have the reflection practice that feels right to you.

- Know that you likely won't see results for a while, but keep trying, it's worth it. Remember, you're doing this for you.
- Start to look for patterns that will help you see the big picture long-term. If you do *x* every time *z* happens, acknowledge and then accept it (more on this in *Chapter Two*). Only then can you choose what to do about it.

Your reflection practice will probably be different every time in the beginning, and that's okay. Some days you might write down a million things that pop into your head. Some days you might just sit and think. It will all help you. It will all make you aware of what's concerning you. You then can decide what to do about it. Remember, like everything in life, the more you practice, the better you'll get. If you struggle with the idea of reflection, try reframing it in your mind. Make it your own. Make it work for you.

It's up to you what you do with the information that comes up in reflection. Acknowledging something doesn't mean you take action on it; it just means you know it's there. Reflection is presence. Eventually, you'll be able to differentiate between what the world wants you to be and who you are.

The power of reflection (Be like water)

The unknown has always terrified me. I feel powerless when I can't lean on knowledge or research as a crutch. The unknown in the context of the potential death of someone I love was excruciating. But consistent reflection pulled me out of the grips of this anxiety. Reflection didn't give me specific answers, but it allowed me to take a step back, which was enough to snap me out of despair. It allowed me to think big picture, long term.

Reflection is a powerful tool with which you can view your life as a whole. Think of your life as a painting. When you're living in it, you can't see the entire picture. Reflection helps you get out of your life for a moment and see it from an outside perspective, as a whole, complex painting.

Humans are extraordinary at enduring, but when you forge ahead with blinders on, you can't see the damage you're doing to yourself. Reflection allows for presence and clarity. It allows you to see that you always have a choice. No matter how challenging your life might be, you can always choose to live in the moment.

Reflection allows you to consciously accept yourself for who you are right now. With a regular reflection practice, you'll get to know the real you, and you'll learn to make choices that align with your values and desires. In some cases, you might simply choose which least negative option, but at least *you* will be making the choice.

By regularly acknowledging who you are, you'll eventually become conscious of your power over yourself. You might not have chosen your circumstances in life, but you do get to choose what you do now. Acknowledgment doesn't change the situation in itself, but it makes a world of difference on the inside.

Start reflecting now. Start feeling your feelings now. The answer is always now. You need to reflect every day, and you need to start now. This isn't easy. The world will tell you that you can't do it now. But the truth, the secret, is that you have complete and ultimate power over yourself, and the best time is always now. If you genuinely feel you don't have time, reflect while you eat, commute, shower—even while you're on the toilet. You are the only thing stopping you from taking back five minutes for yourself.

And remember, if you're stuck, start with emotions and end with gratitude. There is no wrong way to reflect. All you're doing is taking time to listen to yourself, the authentic you.

Breakfast is about gaining a sense of belonging in yourself. Externally it's about being water in its steam form. Steam exists no matter the container, others and the world do not matter. If someone or something tries to hurt you, it goes right through you. By internally acknowledging what's within you, you take the first step to fulfillment. Fulfillment allows you to externally let the obstacles in your life pass through you. "Acknowledgment" externally is like having perspective when a bully says something cruel to you.

It was never about you. It reflects them. Instead of becoming defensive or offensive you accept them, you agree with them, and let them go through.

Once you see and hear yourself you can accept yourself and eventually love yourself. And when you love yourself unconditionally you are unstoppable. The first step is to reflect consistently until you make it a habit. The next two chapters will get you from reflection to loving yourself. There are no shortcuts. Creating your system requires lots of trial and error and hard work, but reflection is the first step, and the best time to start is now.

A reflection session

I messed that up, I think, as I brush my teeth.

Earlier that day, someone said something unpleasant, and I overreacted.

I stop brushing my teeth. *What are you feeling?* I ask myself.

I'm angry. That person said that awful thing to hurt me, and I said nothing.

I want to scream from the frustration of feeling weak. And so, I let myself feel angry for a minute, and after I finish brushing, I go and scream into a pillow.

I feel better.

Why did I get so upset? I now ask myself.

I secretly feel like what was said might be true.

What if it is? What's the worst-case scenario?

Nothing changes physically. I'll accept that I'm potentially that awful thing, but I'm not just one thing but many things, and I love myself holistically. More importantly, I'm enough right now. Even if I am that thing, I've made it this far in life despite it, so it must not matter all that much.

Do I want to improve it?

I could improve if I invest time, but is it worth it? I'll have to give this more thought later.

The anger is long gone now, and I've realized that the things people say hurt me because I let them, because I secretly think about them already. I must address these things. They're either genuine and simply a part of me, or they aren't true and I can ignore them. Either way, I need to feel my emotions first so I can make the choice.

Next time, what's something different I can try?

I'll focus on "listening to understand," and if I feel angry, I'll take a moment to acknowledge to myself that I'm feeling this way before speaking. I'll take one minute to feel and think before doing. Being angry is just an opportunity to understand more about who I am and what I fear. People only hurt me because I let them.

Takeaways

- Reflection is about acknowledging who you are and what you're feeling.
- When building your reflection practice, start small and be consistent. End each session with gratitude.
- Remember that emotions are simply information.
- Keep trying new things, keep what works, and leave the rest.
- You can feel fulfilled in yourself in this moment.

Questions for reflection

- What happened?
- Why did it happen?
- How am I feeling right now? What emotions are present within me?
- How can I process these emotions in a healthy way?
- Why, why, why?

CHAPTER TWO

ACCEPT YOURSELF

Accept your emotions and you will move oceans.

Focus: A key to unlocking your fulfillment is self-acceptance. That's what we'll address in this chapter. With a daily reflection practice, you'll start recognizing patterns and gain a deeper understanding of yourself. When you understand yourself and accept all the parts of you, you'll be able to embrace yourself holistically. This is a need in all of us, but external sources cannot fill an internal need. It needs to come from within yourself.

Story

I could die, I think. It's the scariest moment of my life, but I'm not frozen in fear—I'm energized with awareness. The next few seconds could very well be my last.

My girlfriend and I had just arrived in the bustling city of La Paz, Bolivia, and we were at an Internet café. My girlfriend was applying to graduate school. I'd joined her because we'd agreed to "splurge" and get sushi after (we were backpacking after college and on a shoestring budget, so sushi was definitely a splurge). I had no idea how long she'd need to spend on her application, but I was willing to take my chances for sushi.

After checking my email and surfing the web, I grew bored—social media hadn't yet progressed to the time-suck it is today—so I left all my stuff with my girlfriend and sat on the steps outside the café to people-watch. There was a bustling market outside, and people-watching was a favorite pastime of mine while traveling. Doing so helped me learn about a place and what everyday life there might be like.

It was bright out, so I tried to put on my sunglasses, some knock-offs I'd bought on the street in Peru. My girlfriend had recently sat on them. I'd taped them together, but they barely stayed on my face. After several failed attempts to keep them on, I put them back on my head.

I'd made reflection a habit in high school, and I figured now would be a good time to do some. I thought about where we'd just come from—the salt flats of Uyuni. They were beautiful and unsettling, had made us feel tiny. *I like feeling tiny sometimes. It gives me the courage to go out and do things.* I was struggling with the question of what to do with my life, but when I placed this question against the mass of the cosmos, it stopped feeling that significant.

Earlier in our trip, the travel company we were touring with left us behind in a tiny village on the outskirts of the flats. My toes ended up hurting so badly I wondered if I had frostbite, and I was subjected to a song for so many days that it burned a permanent place on my brain. *That's travel*, I thought. *No matter what you plan, the outcome is always unknown. You need to simply follow the flow and not get too caught up in details.*

Once, while studying abroad, I'd had a gun put to my temple. Definitely one of my scariest travel moments. The guy told me to give him my computer, and I'd instinctively said no. Thankfully, instead of just shooting me, the robber said, "Don't make me shoot you." It took only a millisecond for me to snap out of it and gladly give him my computer. I didn't leave my room for days after that. *I'll never be able to go outside again*, I'd thought. I figured it out, though. I learned to trust myself and changed my perspective. I wouldn't let the robber win. He wouldn't take the joy of travel away from me. *Traveling makes you question your life and its fragility, but it also helps you appreciate it.* That's why I was here, traveling through South America.

While I was thinking about all these things, lost in reflection, I was absent-mindedly watching every person who passed. One individual stood out because he wore a parka (it wasn't cold), and his eyes seemed bloodshot and puffy. I peered at him more closely as he gestured to two friends. They seemed hesitant. He brushed them off and ran inside the Internet café.

I thought nothing more of him.

A few minutes later, I felt my sunglasses being yanked off my head. I whirled around and saw the guy in the puffy jacket. He leaned in, looked me straight in the face with a big smile, and said nothing. It was all very creepy, and my senses were immediately on high alert.

Calm down, I told myself. *He's probably confused me with someone else.*

So that's what I said, in Spanish (the whole interaction was in Spanish).

> Me: You've probably confused me with someone else. Please give me back my sunglasses.
> Confusing Thief: Why?

I take a second to assess the situation. He has one hand behind his back. This is concerning. My mind races to the worst-case scenario: *He has a gun.*

Don't lose your cool, I tell myself, taking a deep breath. *Don't assume the worst.*

I try not to think about the potentially dangerous thing behind his back.

Focus on what you have power over. Try again.

> Me: I don't know you.
> Deranged Stranger: What time is it?

I frown. I'd stopped wearing a watch after mine was stolen on a previous trip. He gestures to his wrist. I show him mine—no watch. A bad feeling starts creeping up. Dread. I need to trust my gut.

No more talking.

I need to get up slowly and return to the café. He can keep the sunglasses. But before I can stand . . .

> Space Cadet: Do you want your sunglasses back?
> Me: Yes.
> Space Cadet: What will you give me in return?

I have nothing to offer—except a small knife in my pocket. I keep resisting the urge to grab it because that would only make things worse, especially considering his two friends are now standing behind him.

> Baked Oddball: Give me money for the sunglasses.
> Me: I don't have any on me.

By this point, I'm totally thrown off. He's still leaning in. This might just be the weirdest robbery in history. I need to leave. I resolve to get up and back away slowly, but my fear has begun to sink in and is making my feet heavy.

Act *now*! I tell myself. This proves difficult. Because I'm sitting on a step and he's leaning forward, I can't get up without moving awkwardly or pushing him. I have to try talking one more time.

> Me: You can keep the sunglasses.
> Worst Robber Ever: I don't believe you. Show me your pockets.

He insists that I pay him for the sunglasses and wants proof that I don't have money.

> Worst Detective Ever: Where's your wallet?
> Me: I don't own a wallet.
> Worst Detective Ever: Then show me your pockets.

There's no use continuing the conversation. He's trying to rob me in broad daylight in the middle of a market. I awkwardly get up and back away slowly. The fear is ready to burst out of me.

Just as I'm about to stand fully, he thrusts his arm forward and stabs my leg.

I blink. What just happened?

I'm calm and scared out of my mind simultaneously. Adrenaline kicks in. Time is going in slow motion.

What am I supposed to do now?

I'm holding my knife. I don't know how it got into my hand. I must have instinctively pulled it out. The thief has what seems to be a boning knife.

I think back to my martial arts training. *What would my sensei do?* He taught me to run—to never fight unless I had no choice. But I can't run. I've been stabbed in the leg. I think that qualifies as "having no choice."

I hear my sensei's voice: *When you must fight, fight as quickly and as brutally as possible, then run.*

What had my sensei said about knife fights? *Plan to get stabbed.* Check. What else? *Try to get stabbed less than the other guy.* Okay. What if there were three guys? I should have stuck with my training longer—I never had the three-against-one lesson.

Then a weird thought pops into my head: *How do I have so much time to think about all this? It must be the adrenaline.*

I have to trust myself, but what I was taught could kill these guys, best case. Just days before, the U.S. embassy was sent packing out of Bolivia. I could quickly end up in prison with no embassy to aid me if I kill someone. They could easily lock me up and maybe forget even to ask questions. What should I do? What move would be least likely to kill?

Time is going so slowly. Or my mind is thinking at the speed of light. Either that or the thief is so high and everyone in the vicinity is so shocked that they're just standing there watching as I think all this through.

I start to question myself. I'm going into freeze mode. I need to do something. My past experiences have taught me that a lack of action always means a lost opportunity.

Think it through but don't overthink it, then act.

I decide to be defensive. I don't want to hurt him, but I'll defend myself if it comes down to him or me. I might end up in prison, but I'll still have my life.

I don't want to die over knockoff sunglasses.

I take a defensive stance and look the guy in the face.

> Me: Now what?
> Jumpy Stabber: What about your leg?

He gestures to my limb. It's gushing blood, but I feel nothing. The adrenaline is great for that, too. I'm hyper-focused.

He could do a lot worse if he hits an organ, I think. Be ready. Focus on him and those behind him. Staying alive is priority number one.

I shrug, as if to say, "I don't care about what's happening to my leg." Then I gesture to him, as if to ask, "What are you going to do now?"

He looks confused. He looks back at his friends. They look even more confused. I get into position and prepare for the worst. Suddenly, the friends run away. At least I have better odds now. And then, to my relief, they return a moment later and pull Parka Guy away. In an instant, they disappear into the crowd.

What now?

I look down to find a pool of blood spreading. I have an audience by this point.

> Stranger: Did you know that guy?
> Me: No, I didn't. He stabbed me. He was trying to rob me.
> Another Stranger: You seemed to be doing an awful lot of talking with someone you didn't know.
> Me: I was trying to talk my way out of it.

Stop, this isn't helping, I tell myself. I go back into my mind, but now the pressing danger is no longer there to keep the fear out. What should I do about my leg?

> Insightful Stranger: Your leg is stabbed. What are you going to do?
> Law-Abiding Stranger: You should report it to the police.

I could go to the police, but they might arrest me and ask questions later.

> Aspiring Administrative Stranger: You should go to the hospital.

If I go to the hospital, they could force me to report it to the police. I still might end up in jail, but at least I'd get medical attention first. Better, but not ideal.

> Insightful Stranger: You're going to bleed out.
> Me: Is anyone here a doctor?
> Genius Stranger: A retired doctor runs a pharmacy a block down.
> Me: Okay, I'll go there.

Oh no. My girlfriend. I can't leave without telling her.

I try to go inside the Internet café.

> Owner: You can't come in here. You'll make a mess with all the blood.

Now what?

> Helpful Stranger: Do you want me to go inside for you?
> Me: Yes, please.

I give him her name. As I wait, I realize how dire the situation looks—as if someone has been butchered. I don't want my girlfriend to freak out, so I try to clean up all the blood. I ask for paper towels. Everyone stares at me.

> Me: Does anyone have paper towels? Toilet paper, even? Something to clean up the blood?

No one has anything to offer. Frustrated, I start yelling for someone to get me something, anything. My girlfriend later told me she thought I had diarrhea and was desperately crying for toilet paper.

I can see her now. She's coming out of the café.

> Me: It might look bad, but I'm okay. Don't focus on the blood. Focus on my eyes. We need to go down the block and see a doctor to stop the bleeding.

She's calm and cool and just grabs our stuff and heads toward the pharmacy. It suddenly occurs to me that the knife might have been dirty. I remember that we have some miner's alcohol from the mine tour. I mention it to my girlfriend and we stop and pour some on to prevent infection.

Unfortunately, as the alcohol rushes over the wound, the pain rushes in. Worse still, the blood flows out of me even more robustly than ever. We look at each other with horror. We need to rush to the doctor now. After all the confusion, I'm just glad to have a clear goal. Getting to the doctor is the focus—the fear of bleeding out is looming. I keep telling myself not to black out. My girlfriend will have a hell of a time dragging me.

Thankfully, the doctor is great. She takes us in immediately and gets to work but has difficulty stopping the bleeding, so she recommends we go to the hospital. I explain my situation, and she seems to concur. Maybe I was onto something after all. Although she does tell me never to pour alcohol on a deep wound; it thins the blood and makes the bleeding worse.

Sure, I think. *Next time I get stabbed, I'll remember that.*

She tells me that if the next thing she's about to do doesn't stop the bleeding, I'll have to go to the hospital. Either way, it's been a good day—I survived. No regrets.

> Girlfriend: Don't worry, we'll get a taxi and go straight to a hotel. No hostel tonight.
> Me: What, no sushi?

> Girlfriend: You still want to get sushi?
> Me: Yes! I think I deserve it!

Breaking it down

The first chapter of *Breakfast* was about acknowledging yourself (through reflection). In this chapter, we dive into the art of accepting yourself, a crucial step toward achieving fulfillment. You've probably heard the saying, "You're your own worst enemy," and it's true. We constantly fight with ourselves, and the noise of the world only amplifies this struggle.

When we accept ourselves, everything changes.

Accepting yourself means that you can see and hear things more clearly. You'll use the energy that was previously consumed by self-doubt to appreciate the moment, ask the right questions, and choose your path. You'll stop caring about what you should be or what others think, and instead, you'll just live. You'll see that you've come a long way, just the way you are. You'll accept that you are you, not perfect, but enough, and feel satisfied in that.

Don't be afraid to start now, because now is always the best time. You'll always be changing, so you must constantly reflect and accept the new you.

Acknowledgment versus acceptance

It's essential to understand the difference between acknowledgment and acceptance. Acknowledging a part of you means that you see it. For example, "I'm shy." Accepting yourself means that you don't feel *the need* to change that part of you. You can change it if you *want* to, though. The key is understanding that nothing about you is wrong or right; it's always about perspective. By accepting who you are, you can embrace and use your unique qualities to your advantage.

For instance, a client felt that being shy was preventing her from taking advantage of social opportunities, but after a few sessions, she realized that being less vocal had allowed her to become an excellent listener. With this skill, she could become part of social interactions in a way that felt true to who she was.

Accepting yourself is also about seeing the big picture in the medium term. While reflecting on your day, you might acknowledge that you were shy in a particular situation. But accepting yourself means taking into account patterns of shyness—that is, numerous instances. A pattern is something, the same thing, you tend to do in certain circumstances. A pattern is not good or bad. It is a part of you, a part of you to embrace.

If you're having difficulty accepting a part of yourself, visualize a scenario in which you succeed with it. Or think back to an instance where you grew and reached your goal despite this thing. This will help give you a bigger-picture perspective. Once you accept something about yourself, it no longer has power over you, and you can consciously choose whether to let it be or to change it.

The first time I was in a life-threatening situation, I acknowledged that my instinct, when under pressure, is to fight immediately. I could have spent my whole life denying this, but I accepted it. Then, I realized that I wanted to change it. As a result, I learned to stop and think before fighting.

In the story I shared in this chapter, I'd reached a point in my life where I'd come to accept myself, and this allowed me to deal with tough circumstances in a way that was best for me. In this particular case, I resisted my natural urge to fight back with my knife.

Emotions and acceptance

When in doubt, start with your emotions. Just as they can serve as the basis for reflection, they can help you learn to accept yourself. Pay attention to your emotions when they emerge and see if you can recognize patterns. This takes time.

For example, one woman I worked with told me she struggled with procrastination. She wanted to change this about herself. Over the span of months, during which she reflected on patterns in her past, we discovered that really, she always finished things. What she struggled with was the feeling of dread that arose when a deadline someone set for her was looming. She accepted this about herself, that she dreaded deadlines others set for her. Then she decided she wanted to work to change it. Her solution was to break down the bigger deadlines set by others into smaller ones that she set for herself along the way. This worked for her. It felt good to her.

Once you see patterns, you'll likely want to change something or focus on something else, but the truth is that you are the way you are, despite all the things you might try. You need to accept this fully before you can make meaningful change. I had to learn this through what seemed like endless failure before I finally realized that I was the way I was and needed to accept this.

Sometimes it is not simply about accepting an emotion/feeling, but accepting that you want or need an emotion/feeling. Take Charlie, for example. She is a client who claimed she was too nice. In reality she liked to please others (be nice) because of the feeling of acceptance it gave her. She wanted to change this about herself because she felt it held her back sometimes. After a few sessions, we discovered that being nice was not the problem, but about who she chose to be nice to. At the time, she was dealing with a difficult employee. In one-on-one conversations, she'd tell the employee they weren't doing what they'd agreed to. Every time, the employee gave an excuse; Charlie, being "nice," would let it go.

Over multiple reflection sessions on her own, Charlie accepted that she was nice and decided to move on. She still had a stellar reputation at her company, so her niceness wasn't holding her back professionally.

Then we reflected together in a session, and the employee came up again. It turned out that other people on Charlie's team were struggling with this employee, too. Charlie realized that she wasn't actually being a good leader. She was not being nice to everyone else on her team—she wasn't helping them solve the problem. This perspective led her to realize that she was not being nice to herself either.

She took a step back and reflected on the long term, and in doing so, she realized that she had to first be nice to herself. With this in mind, she resolved to bring the issue up to her supervisor and to take an active role in coming up with a resolution that was best for all parties. This was difficult, and it meant that she had to push herself. Ultimately, she felt satisfied with herself because she accepted who she was but was now being "nice" her way. (Ideally, she should embrace the need to feel accepted by directing it toward her consciously chosen circle and excelling in those relationships because of it, more on this in the *Lunch* section.) She just reframed it so that she gave that feeling to herself first.

Acknowledge your emotions. If you feel something, great. Label it. State it out loud ("I am angry"). No need to validate it. The very act of feeling it makes it valid. Then accept it. When you accept it, it loses its hold over you. To acknowledge something is to greet it. To accept it is to invite it into your home (to embrace it is to ask it to move in with you–more on this in *Chapter Three*). You can do this work with emotions you've felt in the past, which will help you learn and grow, but the past can be difficult to traverse. It's far easier to reflect on your emotions now, today. We are emotional beings. You'll likely have a wealth of them to work with.

Remember, there's nothing you need to change. Acceptance is a state of mind. You're like steam externally when you're in a mindset of acceptance internally. You accept everything about you internally. Externally, you just let others and the world be, with no friction.

If you're not sure whether you've accepted something, ask yourself, "How do I feel about it?" If you feel no judgment about it, you've reached acceptance. (The difference between acceptance and denial is perspective. You are able to leave your perception behind with acceptance.) Acceptance might sound easy. It's not. It can be painfully difficult. Be kind to yourself. Keep searching for patterns. Keep going further out. We're all different and have different needs. Once you accept one thing about yourself, it will get easier to accept more things. It takes practice. Please don't dwell on how long it takes to get there. It will take as long as you need.

And remember, acceptance is a step further than acknowledgment. It's not saying, "Okay, I'm shy." If you still feel the need to change it, or still see it as "good" or "bad," you're not accepting it.

Tips for learning to accept yourself

- Start small. Reflect daily for two minutes. During this time acknowledge one small thing and then accept it.
- Initially, you might feel as if you're not progressing. Know that this is normal. Stick with it. Doing small things consistently is the key to considerable medium-term progress. Time + consistent reflection = clarity.
- Start with your emotions.
- Remember that nothing is wrong with you.
- Try not to give too much weight to any one thing about yourself.
- Think of self-acceptance as a lifelong game. The more you accept yourself, the better the equipment, but the levels get more challenging (as you address the most significant aspects of yourself). Know that the problems don't get bigger—you're simply able to see and take on more as your capacity for acceptance grows.

The power of acceptance

Self-acceptance takes discipline and hard work. It's worth it. When we're not constantly fighting ourselves, we can more easily live in and appreciate the moment. It takes the whole of you to be present now.

When you accept who you are, your priorities become clear. Accept these too. Make reflecting, acknowledging, and accepting a habit, and eventually, the patterns will be difficult to ignore. Over time, the haze of the world's noise will lift, and the real you will emerge. Accept this version of you. Outside factors will have influenced the current version of you, and that's okay—that's "nurture." The part of you that just is, that's "nature." Accept that too. You'll eventually be able to distinguish what's truly you: the unfiltered, raw you. Accept THAT you. Once you do, you can become unstoppable. Like steam. No matter the obstacle, it will pass through.

Remember, acceptance doesn't mean you can't change or grow, but it does mean that you don't feel the need to. Start small, reflect often, and most importantly, accept yourself for who you are, imperfections and all.

A reflection session

I'm in the shower.

I feel inadequate and embarrassed, I think.

In a conversation with someone, it was assumed that I knew certain information, and I felt terrible not knowing.

It's okay to feel inadequate and embarrassed, I tell myself.

I let myself fully feel these feelings while I shower. Then I spend some time reflecting and have some more thoughts about the situation.

The feelings stem from my pride. I want to be known for being innovative, but that doesn't mean knowing everything. No one can know everything. That's an unrealistic expectation.

What could I have done differently?

Nothing. There's no way I could have known that information.

Why?

I don't have that person's background, and that person assumed my experience was the same as theirs. That's okay. I have no control over that. I need to focus on myself, which I do have control over.

Is there something I'd like to change moving forward?

There's nothing I need to change about myself. In the future, I can communicate more clearly and ask if I'm understanding someone correctly. There are many things I don't know, but I can always ask and determine mutual understanding.

After spending this time reflecting, I realize that my ignorance could be an advantage. It could prompt me to listen to understand and to ask more questions to ensure clarity.

I feel better.

Takeaways

- To acknowledge a part of yourself is to see it. To accept a part of yourself is to not feel the need to change it.
- Reflect on your experiences, thoughts, and emotions. In doing so, learn to accept all aspects of yourself. It's vital to accept every part of who you are.
- By recognizing patterns in your behaviors and emotions, you can better understand yourself and make positive changes in your life (if you want to).
- Remember that nothing is wrong with you. You can choose to make changes, but first you must accept yourself.
- If you decide to make changes, do so in a way that aligns with the true you.

Questions for reflection

- What have I acknowledged but not accepted?
- Why?
- Is this a pattern?
- What has helped me accept something similar in the past?
- How does this look from a third-person perspective?
- What kinds of positive changes could I make to my beliefs and actions (if I wanted to)? How could I hold myself accountable for making them?

* * *

CHAPTER THREE

EMBRACE YOURSELF

Love yourself as you go along–
you're sure to find that you belong.

Focus: You deserve unconditional love. Right now. And you can give this to yourself. That's what we'll explore in this chapter. It's time to embrace yourself and discover the true meaning of fulfillment. You don't need to wait for some idealized version of yourself to emerge before you can feel fulfilled. By embracing yourself today, flaws and all, you'll enjoy a sense of belonging that you won't find anywhere else.

Story

I wake up in the middle of the night in a sweat, my heart racing, glimpses of a terrible nightmare flashing through my mind. I'm seven, and this happens often. The worst part is that I'm deathly afraid of the dark.

The nightmares started in a good place, like a movie theater, and I'd be with someone I knew, but they ended with that person turning into the devil and showing me a horror film, then chasing me. There was always yelling and a sense of primal fear. I'd startle myself awake and would be terrified to go back to sleep. I longed to fall asleep in someone's arms, safe.

I was never allowed to enter my parents' room. Sometimes I'd get so scared that I'd sleep in the living room—between the couch and the wall to my parents' room. It was the closest I could get to them without getting in trouble.

Then I was sent to my grandparents' house. I couldn't enter their room either. The nightmares continued.

Since I was always awake in the middle of the night, I had lots of time to think. What had I done to make my parents send me away? Whenever I asked an adult, I wouldn't get a straight answer. My parents often shouted and said awful things to each other and to my siblings and me, but the next day, they'd act as if nothing had happened. I'd feel terrible, though, and would think about it constantly. What was I doing to prompt this response?

While I was still at home, I'd listen to what my parents yelled about and try to pick out patterns, wanting to help. Cleaning was a recurring theme, so I took it upon myself to clean more. It didn't help; there was always something else to yell about, and my parents wouldn't even notice I'd cleaned.

"Why?" I pleaded when I was sent away. "Whatever I've done wrong, I can make it better. Please don't send me away. I'll change." I was ignored.

In Latin culture, family is life. What had I possibly done that was so bad it warranted breaking up the family?

I loved the time with my grandparents, but I couldn't let go of the question of what I'd done wrong. I didn't want it to happen again. What if I was sent somewhere worse?

My dad would visit sometimes, and this would make me so happy. Sometimes he'd hint at taking me home, but it wouldn't happen. Why? What was the problem? I felt scared and alone, as talking about it seemed to upset both my parents and my grandparents. I had nowhere to go for help or support. Meanwhile, the nightmares continued to wake me.

I loved to watch science shows. A problem was always solved in the span of a show, and the science guy explained that all I had to do was apply the scientific method to solve a problem. But if I didn't know what the problem was, how was I supposed to solve it?

Then one night, I decided to face the feeling of despair straight on. I was only nine years old, but I had a sense that it was what I needed to do. After all, nothing could make me feel worse than I already felt. I thought about how I'd felt abandoned for a while and how the feeling had eventually passed. Then I thought about how I wasn't actually happy when I was with my parents—so why did I miss being at home so much? I had no idea. I kept thinking.

I feel ashamed because I was sent away. Why was I sent away? What's the worst-case scenario?

I've done something so wrong that my parents don't want me around.

The very thought was like a punch to the gut. My parents fought a lot but never sent each other away, despite all their anger. So what had I done? Could I get to the heart of the issue despite having no answer?

Then it came to me. It all boiled down to love.

In the movies, parents loved their children no matter what. Something had happened, and maybe it was my fault, but that shouldn't matter.

I should still feel loved. I don't. And that was the problem beneath all the other problems. That was the issue I had to tackle—feeling loved again.

I was exhausted from thinking about all this, and my conclusions were heart-wrenching, but somehow, I felt better.

So, maybe they don't love me. I don't know why. Maybe they do. But their actions don't make me feel that way.

One night soon after, I thought more about the idea of love. I loved playing with my toys, but this was an empty love. I wished they could make me feel that sense of warmth that being loved brought. Maybe I needed something to protect me, so I wouldn't feel love again and get hurt. Then a different thought came to me. I didn't want to stop loving, but I couldn't control others. That meant I needed to find something that would always love me. I needed to think outside the box.

God loves me, I thought.

I could love God back. He always loved everyone, so he wouldn't hurt me. I felt a little better, but I needed something more. I needed something in the world that would love me.

For several nights I thought about who or what might fit my criteria for loving without hurt. A person who couldn't hurt me didn't exist. No matter who they were, I had no power over them, and one day they could hurt me. And my toys and God didn't give me the same feeling of love I got from other people.

Finally, it came to me. *I love myself*. It was a strange thought. Of course I loved myself.

Did I?

Maybe I did or maybe I didn't, but more importantly, I had control of myself. It seemed like a good place to start. I would love myself.

The idea seemed simple, but it turned out that learning to love myself was a process. First, I had to get to know myself. Who was I?

I'd ask myself a question, and it would usually lead to many others: *What do I love about myself? Why do I love this about myself? How do I build on this*? I felt like a novice at the bottom of a mountain I needed to climb, but I was no longer scared. That feeling was an improvement. What did I have to lose? I'd try it. I'd seek to love myself. To love myself, I needed to see myself. I also needed to believe I deserved to be loved. Then I needed to allow me to love myself, despite everything.

Who am I? Maybe I'm someone who messed up, but it was my parents' choice to kick me out of the house. I always did what I felt was right.

This revelation made me feel warm inside. I was unsure if this was love, but it felt right. I could start here. I could feel good and loved if I believed in what I did, no matter the outcome. It was about how I felt about me, not about what others thought.

The day I understood this, a switch flipped for the better. It would take many years to truly, unconditionally love myself, but that day, my life changed. I felt fulfilled, just being me.

Over the years, I came to understand that love couldn't hurt me because it came from within. I learned to believe in myself and gain the courage to not let myself down despite what others thought. I learned to stop doing things so that others would love me and instead did things that showed me I loved myself. I learned that even if others hurt me, my love would be there to catch me. I learned that my love would give me the strength to love others as well.

After my revelation about love, I still felt terrible about the idea that I might have done something to make my parents send me away. So I felt it. I allowed myself to feel terrible. And in doing so, I accepted it. Then I focused on why I loved myself despite this. I considered the flip side—I felt terrible because I cared. I loved myself for caring. I couldn't make my parents love me, but I could love myself. With this, I was able to let the painful feeling go. It no longer loomed large in my mind.

Loving myself gives me the strength to face anything and everything. Nothing can take my love away from me.

Breaking it down

Chapter One of *Breakfast* was about reflecting on what's happening in your life and acknowledging it. *Chapter Two* was about noticing patterns through reflection and learning to accept the various parts of yourself to the point where you no longer feel the need to change them. This chapter is about embracing every part of you unconditionally.

You belong in yourself, in your body and mind. You can feel fulfillment just being you.

It's important to remember that unconditional self-love is a process, not a destination. It requires patience, consistency, and a willingness to accept yourself fully.

You are enough right now, just the way you are. You deserve to love yourself unconditionally right now.

What does it mean, exactly, to love yourself unconditionally?

To love yourself unconditionally is to embrace everything that you are without judgment or criticism—without conditions. It means accepting all parts of yourself, even the parts you don't necessarily like, and recognizing that each one is an essential component of who you are.

When you love yourself unconditionally, you find fulfillment within you. You become like steam externally. No matter what's thrown at you, it goes through you. Life might change and become complicated, but if you move steam from a cup to a bowl, the essence of the steam doesn't change. You still love yourself no matter what.

You are you. Once you love yourself just the way you are, no one, nothing, can take that away, and you can live in the now. This is the most important ingredient in *Breakfast*.

When you love yourself unconditionally, you stop seeing aspects of yourself as good or bad. You embrace it all and allow your belief in yourself to propel you forward. You stop fighting the current and start working with it. You can use every aspect of yourself, in the right environment, to help you grow. Your love will fuel you from within and make the worst-case scenario bearable. Of course, you will still fail, struggle, and feel pain, but you can always pick yourself up with your own hand. Self-love is vital to fulfillment.

Emotions and unconditional love

We've looked at how acknowledging and accepting your emotions can help you identify patterns and understand yourself better. This, in turn, can help you embrace yourself more fully—and love yourself unconditionally.

Right now, in this moment, you can reflect on your emotions and acknowledge them. Then, doing further reflection, you can look for patterns that reveal the true you. Once you accept these, you can embrace them. Let's look at a specific example.

During reflection sessions, a client, Matt, often acknowledged that he was angry. He soon found a pattern: he was very trusting. People took advantage of this, and he repeatedly got hurt. He often dwelled on the situations instead of just letting himself feel the anger. Over time, he figured out how to process this anger. Typically, screaming into a pillow and then reflecting on it was enough. The more he reflected on instances where he was too trusting, the more he realized that his trusting nature wasn't holding him back. It was simply part of who he was.

In the end, he didn't feel the need to change. Being trusting wasn't good or bad. It sometimes led to unwanted anger, but in the big picture long-term, he was being how he wanted to be. He could see how being trusting was part of why he was so successful. He was a salesperson, and his trust in others gave him others' trust in return. This did lead to him getting taken advantage of, but more often it led to higher sales. He embraced his trusting nature.

In our sessions, he resolved to keep trusting others but to start making small changes that would prevent him from being taken advantage of in any meaningful way. For example, he started small. Starting small meant he would still fully trust someone, but just with the small stuff at first. If he got taken advantage of, well, it was small, and if he didn't, then he moved incrementally to bigger things. This would allow him to be himself, not be taken advantage of as much, and still be successful in sales.

Self-love in action

Many people struggle to believe they deserve to be loved, even after working to truly see themselves. Maybe you're one of these people. Maybe you did something in the past that you feel is horrible and unforgivable. Maybe you feel you don't deserve to be loved because of it. But no one is just one thing, no matter how awful. You are a whole human being, with many facets. You are everything you have ever done and will do.

Once you embrace and truly love yourself unconditionally, you can make changes—if you want to. At this point, you'll be better able to determine what will help you and what will hold you back. When working to create change, try focusing on the things that you view as weaknesses only to the point that doing so doesn't hold you back. Focus most of your energy on your strengths. You'll likely find this more motivating. And you might just find that your weaknesses and strengths are often one and the same—it's just a matter of perspective or environment.

For example, a client, Rowen, was a great planner, but he often found himself frustrated because he'd plan at the expense of doing. Through reflection, he acknowledged this and then processed it by writing about it. In doing so he accepted this quality and saw a pattern: he worked well with deadlines. With this in mind, he experimented with using a timer while planning. Once the time was up, he acted at once: he scheduled the meeting or made the phone call. He liked planning. It was who he was. It was a weakness only when he did it with no limit. With a limit it was a strength—he was always prepared, and this helped him excel in his career. He stopped feeling frustrated and started feeling excited to use his planning skills more.

This is the ideal—embrace what you're wanting to change with your whole self in mind. This will allow you to use it to your advantage.

Let's return to the example of being shy. You've acknowledged that you're shy, you've accepted it, and you've embraced it. You love yourself unconditionally. Now you have three options:

- You can let it be. It doesn't matter that you're shy. You don't have to be social for work, and it hasn't held you back in life so far.
- You can work to make a change while embracing who you are now. You take small actions to make this happen. For example, you resolve to go to one social event a week and to speak to a stranger for one minute at the next event you attend. At the same time, you embrace the fact that you're

a great listener—just by engaging with people through listening, you'll be practicing being more social. This is a powerful reframe.
- You can avoid it. If your job requires you to be social, you start taking steps to change your job. You choose to focus on the aspects of yourself that you see as strengths.

None of these options are "good" or "bad." It's always about what's right for you, right now. The more aspects of yourself you embrace, the easier it will be to love yourself unconditionally.

Tips for loving yourself unconditionally

- Be kind and patient with yourself. Just as accepting yourself requires consistent and repeated acknowledgment, loving yourself requires consistent and repeated acceptance. Avoid judging yourself.
- If you're stuck, break it down and focus on just the next small step (reflection, acknowledgment, acceptance, or embracing yourself).
- Recognize you are enough now. Try now.
- Have faith in yourself. You have endured thus far.
- Remember: you are not one thing. And there is no one like you.
- Once you no longer feel the need to change something, reflect on how it has been or can be a strength.

The power of unconditional self-love

The reward for learning to love yourself unconditionally is invincibility, so to speak. The world calls you shy, you say yes and keep going. You know who you are, and you know what you need. Everything else is flexible.

If you fail, you don't have regrets because you're fully aware of your big picture, long term. You fail in a way that's true to you, and when this happens, you pick yourself up, learn, and try something different. It might hurt, but you know you can rebuild.

It might take a lifetime to learn to love yourself unconditionally. What matters is taking that journey. You must go as far as necessary to embrace every aspect of your whole self. Remember, the path you take doesn't matter. What matters is the fulfillment you give yourself along the way. Be present on the journey.

The world can take everything from you, but it can never take the love you have for yourself. You can build anything, go anywhere, and do anything when you love yourself unconditionally. When you love yourself, you will always have enough—you might not necessarily be eating your favorite foods, but you'll feel full.

Unconditional self-love is a powerful force that can help you make positive changes in your life. By focusing on your strengths and accepting your weaknesses, you can leverage your unique talents and abilities to achieve your goals and live a fulfilling life.

As you continue your journey of self-discovery, I encourage you to be patient and kind to yourself. Remember that you're everything you need just the way you are, and that with unconditional self-love, anything is possible.

A reflection session

I'm on my way home from work and feeling sad. I let a coworker present a proposal we worked on together, and it didn't go well. She didn't stick to our plan, and this made her look incompetent. I told her this afterward with the intention of being helpful and supportive, so she could improve.

I acknowledge the emotion. *I'm feeling sad.*

Why?

Because of what I said. It was true, yet it felt wrong to say it.

Why?

I want to be an empathetic person. What I said was honest and supportive, but it wasn't empathetic. I feel awful.

I stop and let myself feel awful for a few minutes, and then I feel a little better. I have the clarity to reflect.

I feel guilty because of how I offered the criticism, but I'm also the kind of person who wants to help others grow. That sometimes means bringing up issues others might not want to hear about. How I go about this could be just as important as bringing them up, though.

In retrospect, I got impatient. I didn't process my emotions, and in turn, I didn't stop and think before speaking. I want to be honest, supportive, and empathetic, but in this instance, I was only honest and supportive.

Has this happened before?

I tend to do this in competitive environments. I'm competitive. I care more about people than competition, but in competitive environments I lose focus and get lost in my emotions. This was a competitive environment. It will probably happen again. It's part of who I am.

Once I accept this about me, I ask myself, *What could I have done differently?*

I could have stopped and processed my emotions before speaking. I could have waited until the competitive feeling had passed.

Think big picture medium-term. What's the point of saying something?

To help.

How could I have done this?

I could have paused and reflected on how I was feeling, and on what the environment was like. Then acted.

What would action have looked like in this instance?

I could have said it was unfortunate we failed and left it at that until the next day, when I would have been in a better mindset to help. During a competition, I could aim to be neutral.

How are you feeling right now?

I feel disappointed that I let my emotions overwhelm me in a competitive environment. I'm also feeling proud of myself for saying something because I cared. I don't need to change this part of me. To be true to myself, I need to take time and think of the big picture medium-term.

What will you do the next time you're in a similar situation?

I'll take a minute and assess whether rushing to say something is worth the cost, especially considering my environment. Usually, taking one extra minute won't have any real consequences. I'll embrace being competitive and also embrace the knowledge that if I don't take time to reflect while in a competitive environment, I may say something hurtful. As well, I'm going to apologize to this individual. I must take responsibility for hurting others and do my best to make it right.

Takeaways

- Through reflection, embrace everything that you are without judgment. You can thrive because of everything that you are.
- When you love yourself unconditionally, you'll find fulfillment within. You'll be unstoppable.
- Learn to stop seeing aspects of yourself as good or bad. Reflect on how both your strengths and weaknesses can be used to your benefit.
- You are not one thing but a multifaceted person. Embrace what you want to change with your whole self in mind.
- Remember that you are enough as you are now. You deserve to be loved.

Questions for reflection

- Do I believe I deserve to be loved?
- If I were my friend, what would I say to me if I were struggling to love myself?
- In what ways can I prioritize my needs and desires while also being mindful of others?
- What do I feel the need to change about myself? Why? How can I embrace these things and use them as strengths?

* * *

FINAL THOUGHTS

Within action is our satisfaction.

Reflection isn't about finding answers but about gaining clarity and being present with your authentic self. Still, it's okay to struggle with reflection. Spending time getting to know yourself isn't easy. The key is to reflect consistently and keep trying new ways of going about it. This will help you create a reflection practice that works for you.

You can reflect anytime, anywhere, even if you only have two minutes. You have control here. It's your time with yourself. Make the things that work for you into habits. The things that don't work can be viewed simply as information as you tweak your reflection practice. Nourish and enjoy yourself along the way.

Here's a summary of what we explored in Chapters One, Two, and Three:

- Fulfillment comes from within. Reflection allows us to uncover it.
- Make reflection a habit. Be consistent.
- Acknowledge your emotions. They're information.
- Look for patterns and accept yourself.
- Embrace who you are and love yourself unconditionally.
- Life is a journey. You can feel fulfilled throughout it.

Remember that there's no one like you. With a personalized reflection practice, you can adapt to life's changes and feel fulfilled. Keep trying new things. Always remember that you are enough right now.

PART TWO
LUNCH WITH CONNECTION: MEANING

In this part, "Lunch," Chapters Four to Six, we shift the focus to our relationships with others. *Lunch* is all about listening properly, asking for help when needed, and being mindful of whom we let into our inner circle. It's about learning to embrace the people in our lives and love them unconditionally. This is what gives life meaning.

Meaning is a sense of belonging with others. It comes from within. It is also a feeling of satisfaction in choosing who you share your life with, your circle. (A circle is your chosen group of people you feel safe to be your true self with.) You belong in your circle because of the mutual trust, respect, and love. Being your true self in your circle gives you a sense of belonging and satisfaction that allows you to be fully present with others. With fulfillment, we belong in ourselves by ourselves. With meaning, we belong in ourselves with others. (With purpose, we belong in ourselves in the world.)

Through *Lunch*, you'll discover that the key to being present in the moment with others is creating meaning in those relationships. In doing so, you'll find more satisfaction within your connections—and in your life right now.

CHAPTER FOUR

LISTEN TO UNDERSTAND

If you listen to understand, you'll always have a helping hand.

Focus: In this chapter, we'll explore the power of listening to understand. When we listen to understand, we set aside our biases and judgments and focus solely on understanding the other person's perspective. This creates space for connection and empathy, leading to more meaningful relationships. Of course, it's easier said than done. The first step is to listen to ourselves. When we can reflect on and process our own emotions and experiences, we can develop the self-awareness necessary to truly listen to others.

Story

While at my parents' house for the holidays one year, I was sitting on the couch contemplating whether to listen to my book or watch TV when my father entered the room. He had his arms open and wanted a hug. I reluctantly obliged. It was bizarre, but it wasn't the first time he'd done this. The first time, I immediately thought, *Has he been diagnosed with a deadly disease? Does he have only days to live?* What made his desire for a hug strange is the fact that during the first two decades of my life, my father never hugged me.

After our hug, he sat on the sofa and started talking about the past. I sat down again hesitantly, not knowing where the conversation would lead—or even wanting to stay—but I resolved to listen to understand. At this point, I loved myself. He could no longer hurt me. I could be present and love him in my own way. And that day, loving him looked like listening.

He kept talking about the past. Suddenly, he asked for my forgiveness for everything he'd done in my childhood. It took me by surprise, and it was hard to remain present in the conversation and not to return to my mind.

I can't remember certain parts of my childhood—I think I blocked them out. Over the years, people have filled in some of the blanks. My earliest memories are rooted in anger and confusion. The physical abuse started when I was young.

One of my father's most popular punishments involved kneeling. When I was young, I had to kneel and think about the wrong I'd done. As I got older, the kneeling got harsher—from rugs to concrete to gravel. The tiny rocks would cut into my skin not for minutes but hours. Sometimes, I'd have to kneel from the time my father got home from work, around 2:00 p.m., until bedtime, at 8:00 p.m.

While kneeling, I had to think about how the punishment was my fault: *I did something wrong and forced my father to do this*. Part of me believed this when I was younger, so I tried to improve. As I got older, I realized that I couldn't be perfect and that he was choosing to punish me this way. I got angrier. The punishments got crueler.

During one version of the kneeling punishment, I became aware of a psychological element. I had to choose two paint cans and then hold them out, as if I were on a cross, as I knelt. Choosing the cans was daunting. I'd wonder whether to choose lighter ones, to make it easier on myself, or to choose heavier ones, to prove to my father I was strong. It always ended the same—I'd pick the heavier ones and end up with almost unbearable burning pain in my shoulders. I'd be determined not to give in, to show him he couldn't break me. By the end I could barely lift my arms.

Usually during any punishment, he'd lecture me (and my siblings), talking about his childhood punishments. He'd tell us he was being kind to us by not beating us with a stick, as his father had done to him. It was always the same stories, and I'd stop listening. Instead, I'd fantasize about horrible things—things bred from hate, anger, frustration, and fear. I'd become consumed with the hope that I could hurt him one day.

As I grew older, I grew wiser and realized that he was punishing me this way because of the things he struggled with. Instead of dealing with them, he was taking his pain out on me. His drinking and cruelty were the results of his fights with his demons. Still, my feelings of wanting to help him and be "good" always faded into anger at the injustice—and hate for my father. All of this left scars, and only by accepting and loving myself was I able to stop myself from lashing out at him.

Now, as I sat on the sofa with my father, I was just sad. He'd been doing what he'd been taught. He'd never reflected and come up with an answer for himself. My dad was a simple man. He believed in the way he'd been taught, in the idea that if he did what he was told, he'd get hugs and kisses.

He started to ask for hugs when I went off to college. At that time, I resented him. I felt he should be thankful that I even chose to stay on speaking terms with him. Still, I never refused him. That wasn't who I was. I helped others. Doing so gave me inner satisfaction.

One of the punishments I resented the most involved eating a chili pepper. My father would make me pick a chili from the garden and eat it in front of him. He claimed that by allowing me to pick the chili, he was being gentler. They were all spicy, I eventually learned. I particularly hated this punishment because it hurt me with something I loved—food. I was chubby growing up, and in my culture, that meant relentless teasing, but despite that, food gave me comfort. In college, I finally had the mental space to reflect on this, and I realized that the chili punishment was so awful because it created fear and pain around something I ran to for safety. He took one of the few things that gave me joy and made it cause me pain. Through reflection, I worked through my anger around this. My father's parents had punished him in a similar way, and he believed his parents had done right by him.

I love cooking, and nothing can take that away from me. I know that now. But the journey of taking it back was long. Now, he was asking me to forgive him for this punishment specifically.

The worst punishments were the beatings, especially when he used the buckle. My father didn't exist in those moments. I didn't recognize him. Usually drunk, he'd appear to tap into some repressed darkness—pure hate or frustration. My physical pain was intense, but I saw the real pain of my father in those moments. His fear of facing his demons was far worse than my pain. He was like a child who hurt others in a misguided attempt to deal with his emotions. One time he hit so hard that the buckle flew off and hit his stereo. The beating only got worse from there. His music was sacred to him.

When he was drunk, music was the only thing that calmed him. It seemed to take him somewhere else, somewhere he could be free. Often when he drank, he sang. When "we" broke his stereo, we took away his only emotional outlet.

Once again, as I looked at him on the sofa beside me, I was filled with loving sadness. He didn't want to punish us but felt it was his duty. Truly. I think he wished for so many things and never got them. With alcohol and music, he could numb it all and forget.

As I sat with him, remembering my childhood punishments, I understood that he showed love by doing his duty. And to him, that meant to provide and to hand out discipline. He'd expected the reward to be love, the way he wanted it (with hugs), and instead, he usually got hate. He was probably constantly frustrated. Rather than reflect, feel, learn, and try something new, he just redoubled his efforts, and all he got was the opposite of what he wanted.

The punishment that left the most extensive mental scar on me was the showers. If I cried uncontrollably, that type crying where you hyperventilate and sob out of panic and desperation, he'd force me into a cold shower. When I felt scared, angry, or powerless, I cried. Crying was my only way out. Even when I was young, I understood that crying was an effective emotional release. The cold showers took away the last thing I could do for myself. When you cry and get thrown into a cold shower, you stop crying. You can't think of anything but breathing. It feels like being electrocuted.

I didn't reflect on this punishment until college. At first, I didn't know what to make of it. Reflecting on it left me more confused. Over time, I realized it hurt me the most because this act wasn't discipline but cruelty. My crying made my father confront what he was doing, and I think he knew, deep down, that it wasn't right. Instead of facing it, he took away my only outlet.

When I was older, family members told me that my father had been crueler to me than my siblings, even when I was a baby. I finally learned that my mother had sent me to live with my grandparents to spare me the pain for a time. I was darker-skinned than the rest of my family, and someone had convinced my father it was because he wasn't actually my father. He couldn't face this idea, so he shoved it deep inside and let it out on me when alcohol allowed. Reflecting on this is what allowed me to see that we usually hurt those who love us the most when we don't reflect on and allow ourselves to feel our emotions. Out of interest (I never believed he wasn't my father), I got ancestry tests for my whole family a few years ago. The tests, among other things, proved I was indeed his.

My father was simple and trusting. He loved deeply in his way and always believed the best in those around him. Forgiving and loving him unconditionally allowed me to see and appreciate this—but only after I learned to love myself unconditionally. I went from "You'd be naïve to forgive him" to "It takes courage to forgive him."

We were still on the couch. I'd been in my mind. I needed to improve at listening to understand. I sat there and increased my efforts. It was the only thing that felt right. He'd always struggled with words, but I was an expert in reading people, and his body expressed regret. He explained that he didn't know why things had gone so wrong in the past but that he now wanted to do something about it. I respected this and, considering my past, understood how difficult it was for him to say this. He was trying to make amends.

When he finished speaking, I told him I'd forgiven him years ago. I just never told him because I realized forgiveness was for me first and foremost. I told him that I understood why, that we all do what we think is best at the time.

He nodded, understanding.

Throughout it all, I'd loved myself, which had allowed me to accept him totally and, over time, love him in my way. My love didn't excuse his actions, but loving my way gave me inner satisfaction. It gave meaning to my life.

Breaking it down

Listening to understand is a valuable tool in our relationships with others. When you enter an interaction with the intention of listening instead of speaking, of understanding exactly what the other person is saying and where they're coming from, you allow connection to happen naturally.

Over the years, I've heard variations of this concept being used in sales and negotiations. Where I first felt the true power of it, though, was as a coach. To do my job well, it's critical that I listen to my clients to understand them. If someone feels listened to, it's easier for them to let down their walls. And when clients let down their walls, I'm better able to help them.

It takes practice, and it must be authentic. Before you can listen to understand, though, you must listen to yourself. Our emotions can cloud our minds and make it almost impossible to listen. This was what I struggled with while sitting on the couch with my father that day.

The power of listening to understand lies in its ability to quiet the voices in our heads. If someone you're talking to feels heard, the voice in their head shuts up. In turn, this makes it easier for them to listen to you.

While I can offer suggestions to help you improve your ability to listen to understand, the true skill comes from self-awareness. Trying to listen to understand can be like trying to have a conversation with someone while a child is screaming at you for attention. But if you build a good foundation within, through reflection and self love in *Breakfast*, you can get better at listening to others. Be kind and patient with yourself. Again, it takes practice.

The importance of others

In a world where isolation is becoming more common and independence is seen as a virtue, know that it's okay to want relationships. We are social beings. A cake might not *need* frosting, but it's better with it. Similarly, life tastes better when shared with someone else. Fulfillment is self-satisfaction from within. Meaning is the inner satisfaction that comes from doing things for and with others.

Take care of yourself, and then seek out others. Others make everything more. Another person cannot make you happy, but joy feels stronger when shared with someone else. We must recognize our human desire for connection and accept it for what it is.

If you want meaningful relationships, you must invest sustained time and effort. It takes work, but it's worth it. Even just one healthy relationship will give meaning to your life. Reflect, listen to understand, and put in the work. In working to connect with others, you allow yourself to be present in the moment.

What really helps me—and many of my clients—build and maintain meaningful relationships is to set aside time to regularly check in with people, one-on-one. For example, my partner and I sit down and check in with each other for an hour every week. We talk about how we're feeling, what we've been struggling with, and what we need help with. We do this with the long term in mind (How can we help each other grow?). We also meet for thirty minutes weekly to go over the logistics for the upcoming week or month, with the medium term in mind (such as scheduling and planning being social with others). Lastly, we meet daily for two minutes before bed to go over our schedules for the next day, with the short term in mind (What do we need now?). And we approach all these conversations with the intent to listen to understand each other.

Find what works for you. Ideally, as you build meaningful relationships, you'll end up with a network of individuals who walk alongside you—who make the hard times a little easier and the good times a little better. A circle of people who motivate, support, and inspire you. To achieve this, you need to put yourself out there and seek interactions with others. It's always easier not to do this. The fact is, it's scary and requires vulnerability. You may get discouraged. Keep trying. The trick is to always be open to connecting with others.

Again, it's worth the hard work. Others will give meaning to your life.

Emotions and relationships

As we've explored, the body communicates through emotions, so pay attention to them. Even when you're with other people, it's important not to ignore your emotions. Feel them, process them, and then communicate them with the other person. Or, if an emotion is too powerful for a particular exchange, step away and reflect. Maybe you need to scream into a pillow or go for a run before you continue the conversation.

We're all different; our circumstances are always unique. The important thing to remember is that once you fully allow yourself to feel an emotion, it stops having power over you and clouding your judgment—then you can choose what you do with it.

For example, if someone cuts me off in traffic, I might feel angry and scream and then let it go. I don't ignore it because I don't want to take that repressed anger home with me to my family. I acknowledge the anger, deal with it, and then assume the best.

If a coworker I trust and respect stabs me in the back, I might choose to go for a run. I know that only after processing the emotion will I have the mental capacity to reflect on the situation clearly. While reflecting, perhaps I determine that I need to work with them tomorrow (short term), that I want to understand what happened and repair the relationship (medium term), and that I want to have a meaningful relationship with this person and maybe I can potentially improve something and avoid similar issues in other relationships (long term). If I meet with my coworker before going through this reflection process, I won't be able to listen to understand because my anger will be screaming at me in my head.

So many of us run from ourselves and, in doing so, act on our emotions without truly feeling them. When we don't allow ourselves to feel, we often hurt those nearby, those we love, and those who love us the most.

When you're on the receiving end of this, you can take it personally or you can acknowledge that it's happening because of what's happening inside the other person. This is also part of listening to understand. Of course, this doesn't mean you should sit there and take it. It's important to protect yourself–you can love someone at a distance if they're hurting you, whether consciously or unconsciously.

You always have a choice

It's essential to remember this. You don't owe anyone anything, even if they love you or are family. In every relationship, you have the choice to interact, or not. You get to choose how you express your love. You get to choose not to invest in a relationship at any given time. You get to choose to walk away. It's okay to prioritize yourself and take time to embrace and love yourself.

In high school, I didn't want to invest in my relationship with my father, and that was okay. I was invested in learning to love myself. Later in life, I chose to express my love for my father through acceptance and listening to understand. I didn't need to give him hugs full of genuine warmth just because he'd changed, nor could I.

Even if you've put in the hard work and have had a relationship with someone for years, you don't owe them anything. The long term is about you. We all change, and if over time you drift apart from certain people, that's okay. Ideally, if you're checking in with each other regularly, you'll adapt to changes over time and more easily spot issues as they arise. Most importantly, keep reflecting and putting yourself first. This might sound selfish—but if you're hurting, you'll end up hurting the other person. It's better to get yourself to a good place so you can address the relationship in a productive way.

Bottom line, it isn't noble to give others your water and die of thirst. Drinking the water first is the only long-term way to have a healthy relationship with someone.

Lunch (others) is important, but it should never come at the cost of *Breakfast* (you).

Tips for listening to understand

- If you're unable to listen, take care of yourself first. Reflect and listen to yourself. See what you need.
- Preface an interaction with any concerns you might have. (Afraid of how young you are, start with "It is probably hard to believe I have the level of experience I have considering my age and...")
- Focus on talking less. Halve the number of times you talk as you get better at this skill.
- Keep your language neutral ("It appears," "It seems," "It looks to me," rather than "Why do you always do that?).
- Slow it down. Pause and think before speaking.
- Mirror the other person's tone and body language.
- Ask open-ended questions (How do you feel? How can I help?).
- Avoid judgment.
- Periodically summarize what the other person is saying and confirm that you've understood correctly.
- Go into the conversation with no goal other than to connect. Enjoy the interaction. Be in the moment.

The power of listening to understand (Be like water)

The best way to gain meaning in your life is to connect with others, and one of the best ways to do this is by listening to understand. It always fosters better interactions, even if the conversations are difficult ones. In the end, what we truly want from connection is to be heard. Listening to understand allows for this, and it helps us maintain relationships and grow with others over time.

I once had to tell a whole office of people they weren't getting bonuses. I was dreading it. I told my employees one by one, and afterward, I listened to each person and ensured they knew that I understood how they felt. No one was happy, but no one got upset, either.

You always have the choice to leave a person feeling better after an interaction, and the easiest way to do this is to listen to understand. You don't have to agree with them. It's about understanding what they're saying and their perception. Confirm that you do by asking. It might initially feel strange, but it can become second nature with practice. After they've spoken, ask if they're done. If they are, in your own words, repeat what they said and ask if you understood correctly. For extra credit, ask the other person to summarize what was said, to make sure they understood you as well.

Again, there's no way to fake this. You must genuinely understand the other person for it to work, and it takes practice. But the reward is massive. When walls come down, new perspectives emerge.

Just as time spent reflecting helps you to love yourself, listening to understand enables you to love others (which is easier if you already love yourself). And embracing others gives your life meaning.

In *Breakfast*, we talked about being like steam externally. In *Lunch*, we're in liquid form externally. Loving yourself unconditionally, you're full to the brim. When you love others unconditionally, you're still full, but the container changes. (Loving others unconditionally gives you meaning, and this allows you to be flexible and not judge others. Like liquid externally is flexible and does not judge its container.) Others offer bigger containers—but it's important to choose a container that works for you! More on this shortly.

Even as we seek out social connections, we must put ourselves first. This way, if another person slashes at us, the water, we remain the same. Listening to understand helps us be more fluid. Water is flexible, and flexibility is a requirement in relationships. The trick is to be flexible in a way that ensures you remain true to yourself at your core. You can determine this through reflection.

The secret is practice. Practice now, with everyone and anyone. A consistent approach to understanding and communicating is the secret to being with others. You'll know you've mastered understanding when you're nonjudgmental with everyone, including yourself.

A reflection session

I just woke up, and I feel terrible. Yesterday, I sold someone something expensive for the first time. I felt good when I convinced them to buy it, knowing I'd receive a hefty commission.

So *why do I feel terrible?* I ask myself.

I'm good at convincing others to do what I want, and they seem to like me for it. This person even thanked me.

So *why do I feel so terrible?* I ask again.

I want to think about this more, but I need to feel the feelings first. I need to feel awful. I focus on the emotion, and after a few minutes, it releases its hold on me and I realize it's good that I felt awful. It means I care about others, even strangers.

Now that I can think clearly, I ask myself, *What's the problem here?*

I'm getting what I want but am unsure if others are. In this specific interaction, I listened to the other person and then convinced them to buy something I thought was a good fit for them based on what they said to me.

What could I do differently?

The ideal would be understanding them and selling them something that I know with certainty they want.

How can I make this happen?

I could ask. I don't want to guess, so I have to listen to understand. But beyond that, I have to confirm with them that I've understood correctly. It might not work, but I have to try. If I still feel awful, I'll tweak something else.

That feels right. I'll try that moving forward.

Takeaways

- Connection with others is essential to our well-being and brings meaning to our lives.
- Listening to understand is critical to building connection with others.
- To be able to listen to others, you must first listen to yourself and quiet the voice in your head.
- Emotions can help us understand ourselves and our relationships with others.
- You always have a choice when it comes to how you interact with others.
- Maintaining healthy relationships takes sustained effort and work, but it's worth it.

Questions to ask others when seeking to understand

- How, how, how? (When in doubt, ask how. This works because how is the most flexible of the five; with others being flexible is key.)
- How did it happen?
- How do you feel about _____?
- How can I support you in this situation?
- What does success in _____ look like to you?
- What are you taking away from this conversation?

* * *

CHAPTER FIVE

ACCEPT OTHERS AS THEY ARE

Learn to be nonjudgmental and you will be monumental.

Focus: To build a strong circle, acceptance is critical. Of course, not everyone you meet will be a good fit for your circle. You must choose wisely—because you can't change people. Look for individuals who share your values and support your vision. Seek out those who are true and trustworthy. In this chapter, we'll dive into the idea that it's not your job to fix people or make them conform to your expectations. To build meaningful relationships, you must accept people for who they are.

Story

It was going to be my first Christmas away from my family. I knew it would feel strange and lonely, but I couldn't pass up the opportunity. This was going to be so much more than a trip abroad—I was going to visit Alex to tell them I loved them.

Part of me felt silly going to these lengths for someone else. After all, I didn't need them. But I wanted them. And I loved them. I needed to make sure I had no regrets, and this meant telling them how I felt. In person.

Reflection had allowed me to see this. To get perspective, I'd often ask myself, "How will you feel about the current decision or situation a year from now?" This usually helped me realize that what I was doing wasn't worth all the agonizing. Or that it was.

In a year, I would regret not having gotten on an airplane to tell Alex how I felt. So I made the trip.

Once I was there, I struggled to find the right time to speak up. There was always something that made it not the perfect time. And then I reflected.

There's never an ideal time for hard things. The best time is always now.

The moment came when we were in their room one evening. It wasn't the romantic setting I'd hoped for, but we were alone. That was all that really mattered. I told them I'd grown to love them, and that instead of allowing our relationship to unfold naturally, as we'd previously discussed (due to the distance and the different paths we were on), I wanted to invest time and energy to give it the best opportunity to grow.

After I'd said my piece, I felt terrified and relieved. And then I saw their expression. It suggested that they'd already known I felt this way but had wanted to ignore it. My terror and relief turned to embarrassment.

"Okay," they said. Then they told me not to leave hairs on the soap bar in the bathroom.

Really? That's it? That's all you have to say?

I started to ask how they felt in response to what I'd said about our relationship, but they interrupted me. "We have to be quiet. My host mother doesn't like noise this late."

I'd known they might not feel the same way, but this dismissal felt worse than outright refusal. When we were at my hostel later, I attempted to bring up the conversation again, but they abruptly said good night and left—as if the whole notion was so ridiculous that it was best not to mention it.

I couldn't sleep. I felt gutted. Sick. Their refusal to acknowledge my feelings seemed to attack the very validity of their existence. The hours I'd spent reflecting before putting my heart out there were my only saving grace. The reflecting had at least semi-prepared me. I'd hoped for joy and had prepared for rejection, but not for this, not for avoidance.

As the sleepless hours passed, I finally grounded myself in the idea that I had no power over others. *I'll do my best to make the best of the trip and just have fun. I did what I needed to do. I can't control others.* I still felt awful, but who was I to judge? I had to trust that Alex had their reasons.

Unfortunately, nothing was the same after that. Throughout the week that followed, everything I did was annoying to them. Everything I did was wrong and brought up in cruel ways. For the first time in a long time, I started to feel insecure. I was usually confident in myself–I reflected and planned and then acted with conviction in everything I did, and that gave me massive amounts of confidence. But this situation was throwing me for a loop. I felt naked and ashamed. It was hard not to start believing I deserved this treatment, that I'd messed it all up between us. It was hard not to believe that if I'd said nothing, things between us would have continued to be "great."

Every night, I had to reflect. And every night, I ended up at the same conclusion: *It sucks, but I did what I needed to do for myself. I did it for me. I put myself first. I feel fulfilled in myself.*

I knew that Alex wouldn't be acting this way if they weren't struggling internally, but I didn't know with what–they refused to let me in. I had to trust that they were doing what was best for them, but I had to keep my distance to protect myself. This wasn't easy, but I fell back on what I'd learned about myself over the years. I kept working to bring my focus back to the moment and appreciating what I had. My fulfillment relied on this. My return flight was weeks away, and I wouldn't waste my time feeling sorry for myself.

But the following week was worse. I'd get an earful about how awful my outfit was, even though I hadn't asked for their opinion. They'd lash out at me for everything I did, even if it didn't affect them. I'd periodically attempt to talk about "it," but it was dismissed every time, so I finally stopped.

It's true that those we love can hurt us the most. Alex knew exactly what to say and how to say it to make me hurt. I briefly considered leaving, but when I brought this up, they said they didn't want me to go. In the movies, it's often the case that during an argument between romantic partners, one person will just leave. Whenever I saw this, I'd wonder why that individual hadn't just waited and talked it out. Often, the argument seemed to be the result of a misunderstanding or unprocessed emotions. So I resolved to stay. They'd have to tell me directly if they didn't want me around. I got things done by asking questions and outlasting the rest. It was my way, and I'd continue to love in my way.

I'm so confused, I thought, as I reflected one night. *But I'm still trying to make the best of it. I choose to wait and have hope. Alex is extraordinary. I have faith in them. I trust they're just going through something. Love is hard work, and they're worth it.*

One day, on our way to a museum with some friends, they were chatty with me for the first time in a while. I relished the change and tried to engage. We hadn't been talking about anything of substance lately. But the conversation quickly devolved, shifting from me asking how they were doing to them being abruptly hostile. The specifics of what they said were particularly nasty and seemed thought-out. Planned. It hurt. Through reflection and processing my emotions, I was always able to bounce back from situations, but I wondered if Alex could in fact cause me real, lasting damage. I finally saw that I needed to draw a line.

"Go to the museum without me," I told them. Maybe that was what they'd wanted all along.

That night at my hostel, we finally had the talk. (I tried my best to listen to understand.) "Do you not love me?" I asked.

"No, I love you."

"Do you not feel our relationship is worth giving our all?"

"No, I do."

"Then what's the problem?"

"The time."

"What do you mean?"

"The timing isn't good for me."

"I understand that. It's not good for me either. But there is no good time. More importantly, I see the potential and rarity of what we have, and I need to try, for me."

For a few minutes, there was only crying. I eventually restarted the conversation. "What do you want to do, then?"

"I don't know. I didn't plan for this. I wanted things to go differently. I need to get a good job and establish my career before finding a partner to share my life with."

"I can understand that. I used to think that way too, but I now believe that it's harder to find what we have than it is to be successful or establish my career. Do you agree?"

"I don't know. I work hard for what I want and am still trying to decide whether to give up on it or us."

"What does that mean for us?"

"I don't know. The timing is all wrong."

"What's the big picture medium term? You love me and see our value, but you're considering focusing only on your career. Why can't you do both?"

"I just don't think I can."

"Why? You could prioritize your career and still consciously and proactively focus on us with what you have left."

"I'm afraid I might not be able to do that. I need to be able to choose my career first—every time."

"So you're afraid of being unable to continue putting your career before us. Does that mean we're done?"

"No, we're not done, and yes, I'm afraid I won't be able to make those hard choices."

"Do you want us to continue to try to have what we once had?"

"Yes."

I shook my head. "I can't. Things have changed, and these last few weeks have been evidence of this."

"I can't have us be more, and I don't want to give up."

"So we're not what we were and we can't go back. And you refuse to allow us to evolve. What exactly are we, then?"

"I don't know."

We were at an impasse. The problem was, in a relationship, it takes two. Both individuals need to be willing to jump off the cliff together. I didn't blame them for how they felt. And I couldn't convince them of my side either.

I asked myself how I'd feel a year from now and decided that we were still worth it. I'd keep going.

Things didn't get better. The physical element of our relationship was there, but I mostly felt used and ashamed. There was a wall between us, and I was so lonely on the other side. Throughout it all, I didn't lie to myself, which was crucial for sleeping soundly every night. I had to be present and feel it all. I was hurting, but I wasn't living with regret. I tried my best to focus on gratitude for the moment.

My last night there, we went out, ate, and had a light conversation. I enjoyed myself. At the hostel later, I selfishly hoped we'd have a conversation that would offer more insight. It didn't come. There wasn't even a goodbye. They just went to sleep and said not to wake them when I left in the middle of the night to catch my early flight.

When I woke, I couldn't help myself—I tapped them lightly and said goodbye. At my touch, they turned away and held on to the sheets for dear life with their eyes squeezed shut. I stood there in the dark, wanting to cry. Deep down, I knew that this was probably our last interaction. It was sad and confusing to be so physically close yet feel so distant.

On the plane, I had nothing but time to think. I was exhausted, but my brain wouldn't let me rest. I had to reflect and process this, to gain perspective and see the bigger picture medium term I had to put in the time and face everything I felt insecure about and scared of. I knew I could handle all the feelings.

I'd done what felt true to me. It had gone poorly, but it had still felt right. I'd known the risks. I couldn't blame Alex.

I felt my feelings. They felt overwhelming for a while. Eventually they faded and loosened their grip on me. Clarity came.

Sometimes being true to you is painful.

When we expect things from others, we often end up disappointed. I'd known this, but living it was oh so painful. I'd never expected heartbreak to hurt quite so much, but the experience was still worth it; it gave me meaning to express my love.

That's love. It's beautiful and brings with it the potential for pain and vulnerability. And it's worth it.

I had done everything right for me. It sucked, but it was how it had to be, and most importantly, I knew that a year from now, I'd have no regrets. I'd done all I could do. The future wasn't up to me.

Breaking it down

Through that ordeal I experienced the importance of embracing what's true to me while allowing others to do the same. We must be selfish and take care of ourselves first. And with that, we must learn to be okay with the fact that others must also be selfish. Once we can do this, we can work to build a circle of trusted relationships, to give our lives meaning.

Building this circle is one of the most important things you can do in life. It should be made up of individuals whom you love, trust, and respect—of people who accept and love you just the way you are, and whom you can ask for help when you need it. People you see yourself being around forever. Don't let life choose for you. Take control and choose your relationships for yourself. If you cannot actively seek out your circle right now, then focus on becoming what you seek in your circle.

It takes two

It's worth repeating: we are social beings who need others. We are more with others. Building meaningful relationships takes work and, often, pain. Pain is a part of life. Ideally, you're choosing your pain and growing in the process of experiencing it. Do not worry about the length of a relationship, instead focus on appreciating and getting the most out of it today.

At the heart of my story is the idea that when it comes to meaningful relationships, you need to accept that you're only half the equation. A successful long-term relationship of any sort requires two people to choose each other and put in the effort. It's easy to get wrapped up in ourselves and forget that we're just half the story. In movies, we see only the protagonist's side. If we saw the film from the love interest's point of view, it would be an entirely different story. You can be correct in your thinking, and so can the other person. Listening to understand allows you to see this.

My relationship with my father taught me many critical things, most of which help me connect with others. Deep down, we're all more similar than different. Conflicts are rarely about one person being right—they're about people not seeing each other's perspectives. We grow when we internalize the idea that more than one perception can be "right."

In the story in this chapter, I was right, and so was my partner. The problem wasn't black or white but gray.

Most problems with others arise from either not *understanding* their emotions, motivations, wants, or needs, or not *accepting* these things.

Growing your circle

In *Breakfast*, we talked about embracing who you are—about being fulfilled in yourself. When you know what you need and are fulfilled you know what you can adapt to in your relationships. In meaningful relationships we can be in the moment with others. Still, it's not easy to build a circle of people you trust and accept and who trust and accept you in return. It requires you to be selfish and take care of yourself first. Again, you must also be okay with the fact that others must be selfish, too. Only then can you work to build a circle of meaningful relationships.

Knowing what you need is critical when choosing individuals to be in your circle. You can learn more about what you need by accepting others as they are and not trying to change them. With practice and repetition (that's the secret!), you'll come to understand what you need from others and find those individuals who will complement you. Ideally, also chose individuals who you want to emulate. (The longer we spend with our circle, the more we become like the individuals in our circle.) Doing this helps you grow, which keeps you engaged in yourself long-term.

For example, I need the people in my circle to be kind and also better than I am at something—this helps me grow and improve. Others need people who motivate them to start doing things, or people who hold them accountable. Everyone is different and we all need different things. With repetition, you'll find those individuals who complement you. Ultimately, some luck is required. To compensate for this, you must constantly put yourself out there.

Exercise

If you need help building your circle, make a list of what's most important to you. The items on your list might be people, things, ideas, characteristics—anything. Take into account your life as a whole. Don't differentiate between your work and your personal life, for example. That goes for everything in this book. We don't want our various "selves" battling each other. Take ten minutes and write down everything that comes to mind.

Next, take another ten minutes and rank each item in order of importance to you. Try not to overthink it.

Then, for the next week, write down what you're doing during every hour of your day. Be specific. The aim is to get a sense of how exactly you're spending your time day-to-day. At the end of the week, compare what you did to your list of what's most important to you. You are what you spend your time doing, so adjust as necessary. The people in your circle should align with what's important to you in some way.

* * *

If someone wants to be fit but dedicates no time to it, they won't achieve that goal. This logic applies to building connections with others. If creating meaningful relationships is important to you, you need to put in the time.

Start small. Break it down. Set a certain amount of time on a weekly or monthly basis to be social, for example. You might start by just showing up to a social engagement you've been invited to. Getting in the habit of simply being there is a great first step—no need to be social at first. Determine when you'll take the next step (maybe after two months, for example), and then take it. The next step might be to introduce yourself to one person at each social event you attend for the next month. Then you take the next step. Do what works for you. What's important is to have a plan for how to progress to the next step.

Time is a tool. You can use it as you wish or let it push you around. When building a relationship, you need to be ready to spend time on this, and so does the other person. There's no shortcut. You must meet people, sometimes a lot of people, build relationships based on what you think you want, and then learn what you need through trial and error. Focus on small steps and be consistent in your effort.

Think back to your most significant accomplishments. You didn't just stumble on them. They took time and work. Thankfully, once you have meaningful relationships in your life, you can focus on maintenance—checking in —which is easier than building relationships. In the meantime, find inner satisfaction in the process of connecting and remember that life is about the journey. And. As I keep pointing out, the journey is now.

We all need at least one person we can trust and lean on. Build from there. If you're finding it difficult to build your circle because you're struggling with trust, start small. Trust them with small things, and as they continue to reinforce that trust, build up to bigger things. If they let you down, communicate that with them and give them another chance. If they do so again, consider walking away—or creating some distance if you love them. With careful consideration, a third attempt can be offered under the right circumstances, but be honest with yourself through reflection.

Tips for growing your circle

- Aim to include people you look up to and who can help you grow in some way. (Helps you grow, and growth helps with engagement.)
- Ensure there's mutual trust and respect. Start small.
- Consider whether you can lean on them in the hard times.
- Remember that you can't change others. Accept people for who they are and expect the same in return.
- Don't be afraid to let someone go if they're not a good fit or they change over time.
- Enjoy the process and be in the moment. The act of connecting with others is satisfying.
- Be kind and patient with yourself as you learn about what you need.
- You will become more like those in your circle—choose wisely.

The power of trusted relationships

When you have a circle of support, you can take on so much more in life. You can only lift so much weight on your own. With the help of another, you can lift more, and with many people, you can lift almost anything. You might just be surprised by how many successful individuals got help along the way.

Your relationship with your romantic partner will be one of the most challenging and impactful ones of your life—invest accordingly. Allocate time to building and maintaining this relationship. When I ask successful people how they've gotten to where they are, the most common answer I hear is "with the help of my partner." If you don't have a partner (and want one), focus on how you can become the best partner possible, to attract the type of person you want.

Like muscle growth, some discomfort is good, but too much pain will injure you. Maintaining good relationships requires constant reflection and acceptance, but not to the point where you allow others to hurt you. With others, the highs might be higher and the lows lower. Embrace it. Be in the moment. Love is work. It makes life more. You and the people in your circle are like chocolate and peanut butter—each is great alone, but together they're extraordinary.

Remember, when you're water in its liquid form externally, others are simply the container. If you're water that's murky, you'll still be murky in a container. You need to be vibrant on your own. Others will complement this. You can adjust to the container, as long as you're full in yourself.

When it comes to relationships, the most important thing to keep in mind is that we must accept others just as they are. And we must constantly re-accept ourselves and the other person as changes happen—or make a conscious decision to let someone go.

Trusted relationships are essential to creating meaning in your life. It takes work and repetition, but with practice, you can find those individuals who will complement you and help you grow. Listen to understand. Seek out what you need. Don't be afraid of trial and error. Strive to connect with others, on your terms. Finally, keep in mind that we tend to project. If you dislike someone, you'll often dislike them for aspects of their personality you dislike about your own. This is part of the reason it's so important to embrace yourself first. Reflect, accept, embrace.

A reflection session

I'm exercising and reflecting.

At a social engagement yesterday, a friend said something unkind about me, and I knew their intention was to hurt me. The comment itself didn't upset me, but I was upset that this person wanted to hurt me. I confronted them privately and they apologized, but they claimed they didn't mean it the way I'd taken it. I sensed that they were lying.

I feel the hurt for a few minutes.

It's still there. I need to do something.

I run for a bit and feel better. Now I have the clarity to try to understand it from my friend's perspective. Looking at the big picture long term, I can see I did similar things in the past.

My friend struggles with being social and was probably just trying to fit in.

What are my choices?

I can assume my friend made the comment with the sole intention of hurting me. Or I can accept that they got caught up in wanting to be liked and hurt me in the process. In my mind, the world revolves around me, and this is fine, but other people's worlds revolve around them. Moving forward, I'm going to tell my friend that I can appreciate why they did what they did and then ask them not to do it again. If they do, I have the right to reconsider our relationship.

I needed this reflection time. I needed to stop, let myself feel my emotions, and then accept the situation for what it was. I needed to remember that there were two people involved in this situation. There were two perspectives.

Takeaways

- We must be selfish and take care of ourselves first. And we must learn to be okay with the fact that others need to do the same.
- Trusted relationships give life meaning. Building a strong circle requires choosing individuals and then gauging if you're a good fit for each other through acceptance—many times.
- Start creating your circle now. Choose wisely.
- Finding people to build successful relationships with sometimes takes luck; try often and consistently to improve your luck.
- It takes two, But you can only control your half.
- Let yourself lean on your circle. With others' help, you can lift more weight.

Questions for reflection

- What is most important to me in life?
- How do I spend my time?
- Who makes me want to be a better person? Why?
- What do I want from others?
- How can my circle help me?

* * *

CHAPTER SIX

LOVE OTHERS UNCONDITIONALLY

Love and embrace and you will gain meaning in any place.

Focus: When we fully embrace others we create an environment of acceptance and growth that allows everyone to thrive. This doesn't mean loving blindly. It's about approaching people in a holistic way, embracing their complexity. In doing so, we can build a foundation of unconditional love. That's what we'll explore in this chapter.

Story

I'm lying on the ground crying uncontrollably—and laughing. My one-year-old, Orion, just farted, and it reeks of death. I made a face and said "Fuchi," and for some reason, this was the funniest thing in the world to them. So I said it again. Again. Every time I take a breath, I say "Fuchi," and Orion giggles with more intensity. I keep laughing and crying. I'm so happy.

I eventually stop because my side hurts and I'm concerned that my child might not be getting enough oxygen. In this moment, I'm present and reminded of how I'll love them unconditionally now and forever. It doesn't matter what they might do or become. They could grow to hate me, or want to hurt me, yet I'll still love them. That's unconditional love: vulnerability with no conditions attached.

I love my child and my partner unconditionally. This means loving them to the degree that I wouldn't be able to stop loving them even if I tried. Unconditional love takes the "should I" out of the equation and instead lets you focus on appreciating that person at that moment as you choose. It's how I was able to love my father. When I was with my father, I was present, showing love my way, loving myself unconditionally. Afterward, I always had to create distance again, but I still accepted him just the way he was. I loved my father unconditionally at a distance and, in doing so, felt satisfied within myself.

In a perfect world, we'd always consciously let someone into our circle before loving them unconditionally, but with family members, this can be trickier (if we want to have a relationship with them). In cases like mine with my father, it's most important to put yourself first. Prioritize yourself. When dealing with someone difficult you didn't choose—such as forcing a relationship in order to enjoy a delicious holiday dinner—pretend the person is four. Listen to understand, but pretend they're four. Seriously, it helps. It works because the secret to dealing with difficult individuals is patience, not judging, flexibility, not taking it personally, curiosity, and not being closed-minded. We tend to do this best with children.

Despite everything I endured in my childhood, I still loved my father unconditionally, and for a long time I hated myself for this. I had to learn to accept and embrace this part of me. For a long time I wanted him to see the pain he'd caused. I wanted him to understand how he was wrong. But this never worked. I'd only end up frustrated. That all changed when I embraced myself. Doing so allowed me to embrace that I loved him unconditionally. The situation didn't change; I changed. It sounds cheesy, but it's true—the moment I embraced myself I was able to embrace him. I stopped trying to change him and simply embraced how he was. This let me enjoy him in the moment for short periods of time.

When this happened it was as if a weight had been lifted. I didn't need to justify my actions, to myself or to him, and that made all the difference. From then on, our conversations were different. I wasn't looking for experiences that would validate my love. Instead, I enjoyed my love. I loved him because I wanted to.

It took a long time to get to this place with my father. I had to do a lot of listening to understand. I had to do a lot of reflecting. But the work was worth it. Interestingly, it's usually when we stop wanting to change another that the dynamic changes for the better. It's all about appreciating the moment. We set aside our expectations and focus only on connecting for the sake of it.

Loving someone unconditionally involves asking yourself, "How can I best enjoy this moment with this person?" instead of "How can I change this or get them to change this?"

Now that my father is gone, I'm so thankful for the moments in which I allowed myself to simply be present with him. They gave me joy and they paved the way for similar moments with my mother, my partner, and my child.

I remember the first time I accepted my partner entirely. It involved tape.

I always dreaded discussing anything that involved my organization and her chaos, but I'd been looking for a roll of tape for an eternity. I knew she'd used it last, so I either had to give up or suck it up and have the conversation. (Take it from me—don't avoid having these kinds of discussions. The problem will only fester. It's best addressed head-on. Don't let tape end your relationship!) The conversation went something like this.

"Where's the tape?"

"Did you check the drawer where we store the tape?"

"Yes," I say, frustrated but trying not to show it. "That's why I'm asking."

"I don't know, then."

"You were the last person to use it, though."

"Are you sure?"

I nod. "You used it for that package you sent out last week. You never put anything back where it goes." I'm having more trouble hiding my frustration now. "I even labeled it with a note about where it belongs. Just in case you forgot."

My partner is also upset now. The word *never* wasn't a good choice (it never is). "I did use it. I remember now."

I take a deep breath so I don't start ranting about the importance of putting things back in their place. "So can you tell me where it is? I've been looking for twenty minutes."

"No, I don't remember. Did you look near the desk?"

"Yes, it's a mess."

"I don't know."

"Fine, then I'm going out to buy tape. You'll have yours and I'll have mine. Please don't touch mine." I actually tried this in the past and it didn't work—my partner would always grab mine because it was easiest to find.

"Stop being a baby. I'll help you look for it."

Seconds later, she hands me the tape.

"Thank you. Where was it?"

"On the desk."

"Where?"

"In the delivery box, under all the mail."

"Why didn't you just tell me that?"

"I only remembered once I got to the desk."

I walk away feeling as if my head will explode. At least I got the tape. What did I need it for again?

Arguments like this had been happening ever since we started living together. This time, I felt my frustration and then reflected on it.

Why do situations like this affect me so much?

I thought about how I was an organized person largely because of my upbringing. (Remember, asking *why* is always a great place to start after you've felt your emotions and are ready to grow.) It hadn't felt good being forced to be organized when I was growing up, and my forcing it on my partner probably didn't feel good for her either. From our own perspectives, we were both right. The only way I could change my situation was to change myself. I acknowledged to myself that I loved my partner in her entirety, not just parts of her. I could still wish she were more organized but I could stop judging her chaos. The joy I got from sharing a life with her far exceeded the compromises necessary.

The day I stopped judging her and trying to change her was the day I truly embraced our living arrangement. To get to this place I had to admit and accept what I felt. I had to let go of the idea of right and wrong and acknowledge the facts of the situation. She was raised in chaos; my parents forced me to be organized. We were the same in that respect—products of our environments. I had to accept this about myself and about my partner. Only then could I appreciate us.

Unconditional love helped me accept her. I already knew I loved her unconditionally; I just had to remind myself so I could accept her without judgment. In reflection, I realized that I'd been trying to shame her for her chaos. I'd been trying to change her, even though I'd told myself I'd never do that. It was a good reminder that I needed to make some tweaks.

The next time a similar situation came up, I didn't judge. (Never judge the present, appreciate and embrace it.) Instead, I allowed myself to enjoy her company as we talked about it. I listened to understand, and then I got confirmation that I'd understood correctly. Then I explained myself and confirmed that my partner understood my perspective. We ended up reaching a natural compromise. Oddly enough, over time she became neater and more organized and I became more chaotic. It was liberating just to be me and to let her be her.

In a way, unconditional love is a "take it or leave it" proposition. In long-term relationships, sometimes you need to remind yourself that you accepted it all a long time ago. Imagine trying to enjoy a fantastic meal while in a heated debate with the restaurant owner about the price. In the end, you're simply trying to validate the cost to yourself. After all, you accepted the price the moment you ordered the meal. Unconditional love takes the price out of the equation and allows you to enjoy the meal. Keep in mind this is just half of the equation—the other half isn't up to you. The restaurant always has the right to refuse service.

Don't get me wrong—I still get annoyed at the chaos sometimes (just ask my partner!). But acceptance makes it more palatable and allows me to feel joy in the moment with her.

We never know what others will do, and this can be difficult. *Will my father stop wanting to interact with me because I'm not showing him love the way he wants? Will my partner be okay with me being so organized? Will my child accept me when they're an adult?* We can't answer questions like this. We can only do what's true for us and keep loving unconditionally. The rewards are worth the uncertainty.

Today, my partner and I are more solid than ever. We tend to move to a different part of the world every few years, and no matter the obstacles, we overcome them together.

You are indestructible when you love yourself. You can be completely fulfilled within yourself. But with the love of others, your journey has meaning. Unconditional love is what gives meaning to my life. I am more satisfied in myself when I do things with those I love unconditionally in mind.

Breaking it down

This final part of *Lunch*, embracing and loving others unconditionally, is difficult. I came to understand what unconditional love truly means only through multiple experiences. It took years to internalize it.

Embracing others gives our lives meaning. Not only do we need others—when we choose our circle wisely, there's almost nothing we can't do. But it all starts with loving yourself. You can love others only as much as you love yourself. With fulfillment in yourself you can consciously connect with others with the energy you have left to give.

When we reflect, accept ourselves, and love ourselves unconditionally, we gain fulfillment in ourselves. That's *Breakfast*. When we listen to understand, accept others as they are, and love those in our circle unconditionally, we gain meaning in our lives. That's *Lunch*.

All of this takes consistent repetition over time. It takes constant tweaks to how you connect with others. And remember, it's all about making changes for yourself. You cannot change others.

Deathbed reflection

My favorite thing to ask elderly people is "What do you wish you'd known earlier in your life?" Many of them say that they expected to have more time to enjoy their relationships with others—and that they wish they'd known this earlier.

If you're struggling with unconditional love, reflect on your death. It will help you understand your life.

Go out and experience connections. Don't wait for the future or get stuck in the past. A million distractions and noises can cloud our sight in the present. Clear your vision through reflection and use that insight to grow and appreciate what's right in front of you. You will get hurt along the way, but it's essential to stay open. Continue to love yourself. Others enhance what you already have within you.

When you're on your deathbed, the future won't matter. Excuses and distractions won't matter. What will matter is the moments you spent with people you loved and the moments you spent doing things you loved.

Putting in the work

Even if you love someone unconditionally, you have to work at the relationship. With this in mind, consider that poor communication is often at the root of most problems we have with others. Use your understanding of people in your circle to guide your communication with them. In other words, try to express yourself in a way the person you're interacting with would appreciate. Hopefully, they reciprocate. Strong relationships are built on mutual respect, a willingness to put in the work, and a readiness to adapt (remember, water in liquid form externally adapts to its container but remains full in itself). Be conscious and ready to walk away if the other person isn't open to build on this kind of foundation.

People and situations change. This isn't good or bad, and it's no one's fault. What's important is to consciously step back from a relationship if either you can't continue to put in the time and effort or the other is unwilling. Removing someone from your circle doesn't mean you stop loving them unconditionally—it means you stop investing in the relationship and in doing so stop allowing them to hurt you.

Tips for loving others unconditionally

- Embrace others holistically (nothing is good or bad).
- Choose wisely who you let into your circle.
- Take care of yourself first—be fulfilled.
- Listen to understand.
- Put in the time and effort—check in.
- Love yourself unconditionally.

The power of loving others unconditionally

Cultivating relationships fueled by unconditional love doesn't just give your life meaning—it can be a lifeline. Ask for help when you need it. Others can offer you the most incredible gift: their time and input. We all have different experiences and perspectives that we can share with others to help them grow. Even strong pillars need other pillars to form a foundation. There are instances where you might reach out blindly in desperation, but when you can, take the time to reflect on your situation so you know what you're seeking and who might best be able to help you.

Know that there are many routes to what you want. Others can help you narrow down your choices and navigate obstacles along the way. And they can walk with you. You don't want to reach the top of the mountain and have no one to share the view with.

Again, embracing and loving others unconditionally is difficult, but it's achievable with constant repetition over time. Start by reflecting, accepting, and loving yourself unconditionally. With fulfillment in yourself, you can consciously connect with others and enhance what you already have within you.

Being open to connecting with others means being vulnerable, which is scary, but the results give your life meaning. So be brave and put yourself out there–the reward is worth it. You are more than able to do this.

You are enough now. Start now. Just a little at a time.

And remember, reflection is critical to progress. No one knows how to do it all perfectly. Only through taking action, failing, and then learning will you grow. Reflect, do, reflect, grow. Repeat.

Through it all, take care of yourself. Make sure you replenish your energy before giving some to others. Empower yourself to be you to find fulfillment. Empower others to be themselves to find meaning.

Clear your vision through reflection and use that insight to grow and appreciate what's in front of you. Don't wait until you're on your deathbed. Don't let distractions and noise cloud your sight in the present. Enjoy your connections now. When you surround yourself with people who love and support you unconditionally you'll have a life full of meaning from within you.

A reflection session

I'm showering and reflecting.

Why did my last conversation feel so uncomfortable? I wonder.

Someone I love unconditionally asked me for help and I'm feeling awkward about the exchange. Uneasy. I'm not sure why, so I let myself feel it for a few minutes.

It makes sense that I feel this way, I think. *The topic wasn't one I usually discuss. Nor is it something discussed in society in general.*

Do you feel uncomfortable because the world says you should?

I start to feel insecure about this and then disappointed in myself.

Why? Where is this disappointment coming from?

When the person asked for help, instead of being supportive, I ended the conversation as quickly as possible. That's not the person I want to be. When someone gets the courage to ask for help, I want to be supportive. It was probably difficult for them to ask.

I take some time and reflect on the best way to be supportive in the future.

When uncomfortable topics come up, I need to take a minute to gain perspective and courage. I was thrown off in this instance, so I ran away, so to speak. Next time, I can allow the other person's vulnerability to help me grow and be more vulnerable as well.

I realize I need time to deal with the emotions and consider how best to embrace this part of this person in my circle. I set a time to reflect on this tomorrow.

Takeaways

- Embracing those in your circle means you thrive with them because of who they are.
- Repeatedly embracing aspects of another person is the best path to loving them unconditionally.
- Meaningful relationships take time and effort. It's worth it.
- Your circle can be your lifeline. Reach out for help when you need it.
- Being in the moment with others gives your life meaning. Enjoy your connections now. Don't wait.

Questions for reflection

- What are some of the most significant obstacles I've faced in my life so far? How have others helped me deal with them?
- How can my circle help me now?
- Am I loving the people in my circle unconditionally?
- If not, how can I embrace them?
- How do they embrace me?

* * *

LUNCH

FINAL THOUGHTS

Be led by curiosity and you will always be at your maximum velocity.

All the suggestions in this book are meant to serve as tools. It's up to you to use them. It's up to you to practice, tweak, and adapt. Stop trying to be "right" and start letting curiosity or understanding lead you. Try things out and then try something slightly different. Try something new every chance you get. And enjoy connecting on the journey. How you get there is up to you.

We are social beings. That means we need connection. You have the power in every interaction with someone to leave them better, worse, or the same. Ideally, strive to leave someone better. It can be as easy as a simple and genuine compliment. One of the kindest things ever said to me was after being sick. Someone I passed every day in the hall stopped me and said they missed me. I laughed, thinking they were joking, but she was serious. But we rarely exchanged more than a couple of words. That short interaction always left me feeling like everything would be okay, and I missed that. I remember that often, even after 15 years. If you are not okay internally, leave them the same. It is best to strive never to leave someone worse.

Put in the time and effort *consciously* and you'll feel more satisfied—because you'll be doing it your way. The secret is to be satisfied in simply trying. You can always be present with others. You can always find meaning.

In summary, here's what we explored in Chapters Four, Five, and Six:

- Being in relationships with others gives our life meaning. Connection is a basic human need.
- Listening to understand allows for deeper connections. It's a powerful tool.
- Accepting others means embracing them for who they are, without trying to change them.
- When we embrace others, we all thrive. And this embracing leads to unconditional love.
- You can do anything with a circle of people who love you unconditionally. Choose your circle wisely.
- Being present with others takes effort and patience, but the journey itself is meaningful.

Finally, remember that you can't control others. Be kind and patient with yourself. Prioritize yourself. Give to others only what you don't need for yourself.

* * *

PART THREE
DINNER WITH PASSION: PURPOSE

In this part, "Dinner," Chapters Seven to Nine, we look at the final element of this guide—purpose. Once we're fulfilled in ourselves and enjoy meaning with others, we can shift our focus to what we do: How we exist in the world. How we incorporate our passions into daily life.

Purpose is a feeling of satisfaction from within you when you do your passion. Purpose is belonging in the world. It feels authentic and true. It is where your why, your how, and what you love to do meet. It allows you to be present in the moment in the world.

Throughout *Dinner*, we'll focus on developing a system that works for you. This will involve trying new things, reflecting on your experiences, and identifying patterns that resonate with your true self. By focusing on your "why" (your direction) and your "how" (what propels you forward), you can unlock your passions and give yourself a sense of purpose now—a deep sense of inner self-satisfaction. *Dinner* is the key to finding purpose in what you do.

CHAPTER SEVEN

START BUILDING YOUR SYSTEM

Be flexible and you will be exceptional.

Focus: In this chapter, we'll take what we've learned in *Breakfast* and *Lunch* and explore how to make it work best for you. It's time to figure out what works for you and create a system around it. Your system is your way of doing things, your unique approach to reflection, connection, and action. It's the set of guidelines and good habits that will help you live the life you want to be living. Whether you're looking to start a new project, change your career, or simply improve your daily routine, a personalized system of doing can help you get there with purpose.

Story

My world was crumbling around me. I was so upset I couldn't think straight.

This is so unfair!

I was nine and living with my grandparents, and my favorite thing to do was go to the movie theater with my grandfather. He usually gave me tasks to finish throughout the day, and if I got done early we'd go to the movies. Earlier that day, he'd told me that we could go see *Apollo 13* if I finished my chores by 11:00 a.m.

It was 10:30 a.m. The only thing left to do was sweep the front and outside of my grandfather's welding shop, but I knew there wasn't enough time, even taking the previews into account. It took me forever to sweep. I'd left it until last because I disliked it and wasn't good at it. So I did what any nine-year-old would do—I swept everything behind the door and then said I was ready to go.

Of course, my grandfather noticed (though nine-year-old me was surprised by this!). And then he told me I had to sweep the whole area again. Now there was no way we'd make the movie.

I was infuriated, but my grandfather, as always, insisted on giving me a nugget of wisdom: "In life, you do something right or not at all."

I wasn't fully listening. All I could think about was that I wouldn't get to go to the movies. To add insult to injury, my grandfather had finished his tasks and was now watching me sweep.

"Who taught you to sweep?" he asked, after a few minutes.

"No one. It's just sweeping."

"Nobody ever taught you how to sweep?"

"No," I said, now confused as well as upset.

"You sweep very poorly and slowly. At your rate, we'll miss dinner."

I ignored his comment, but he ignored my anger and proceeded to teach me how to sweep. I was curious enough to watch him, and after trying it out, I realized it would in fact take me much less time doing it the way he'd shown me. It also brought me great pleasure to do something both better and more quickly.

Why did I expect to know how to sweep? I should have asked for help.

I decided to apply this idea to everything. If I asked questions about everything, I'd learn to do things faster and better, which would translate into doing more of what I wanted, like going to the movies. Worst case, someone wouldn't know the answer. Best case, I'd gain knowledge to better myself.

From then on, I asked questions about everything. Little did I know that I was starting to build my system. After years of asking questions, I learned that questions got me answers but didn't give me results unless I was open to adaptation. If someone suggested something, I had to try it. If it worked, great—I could add it to my system. If it didn't help, I could leave it and move on. And eventually, I learned that I didn't need to know everything; knowing what and whom to ask was more important.

I uncovered the need to try new things while working at my first job out of college. My boss had just called me to talk about a minor mistake I'd made, and once again, I was fuming. *How can they expect me to be perfect?* I was tired, working six days a week, fourteen hours a day.

At the end of the call, my boss had told me not to let the mistake happen again. *How am I supposed to do that?* I didn't have time to double-check my work, as I was being given more and more of it. The better and more efficient I became, the more I was given (a common issue in Corporate America!). The reward for my effectiveness was more work.

I was angry at the company for essentially punishing me for being efficient with my time while my counterparts were doing less and getting paid the same amount. And I was angry at the whole system, stewing about how unfair it was. But after reflecting, I realized I was upset with myself. I felt ashamed that I'd made the mistake. I believed I shouldn't be making these types of errors.

What can I do? I asked myself.

I reflected for a long time but couldn't get over the mistake. It took me days to finally embrace the anger. Only then was I able to let it go and seek a solution.

I was tired. I wasn't thinking as clearly as usual. I'd been on autopilot, to the point of being overly confident and not questioning what I was doing. What could I try that might help? I needed to reboot my brain, somehow.

First, I needed to remind myself that I had a choice. I resolved to apply for at least one job a month. This would help me remember that I was choosing to work at the company. This decision alone made a world of difference. Then, I took some more time to reflect and remembered a study that had shown that naps drastically improve the cognitive ability of pilots. I looked it up and reread it. Next, it was time to incorporate the information into my system.

I started with ten-minute naps, in my car, at lunchtime. I felt awkward knowing people could see me, and the seat was so uncomfortable that I couldn't fall asleep. By the end of the first week, I felt worse. I'd fallen asleep just a few times for a few minutes and had woken up more tired.

After another week, I was falling asleep quickly and consistently but still waking up tired. So the following week, I tried twenty-minute naps. Instead of feeling tired when I woke up, I felt spacey and out of it. I resolved to try one more week, giving myself a month. (For me, a month tends to be a good increment of time to try something. A day or a week can be just as effective for others. What's important is that you believe it's enough time to give an idea a chance.) I reflected and theorized that I was probably falling into a deep sleep during a twenty-minute nap.

So, the next week, I took fifteen-minute naps. They worked! I woke feeling refreshed and clearheaded. I was still afraid of what others would think of me for sleeping in my car, but I couldn't deny the results. I had to be true to myself. Naps worked for me and that was all that mattered.

I kept up the habit, no matter where I was or whom I was with. If I didn't have my car with me, I'd find another place to take my nap. My employees and managers eventually asked me about it. I told them it helped me to do my job better; I recommended it to them. Many were skeptical, and some probably laughed behind my back, but some gave it a shot. After all, I had research and experience to back me up. Eventually, I had a group of nap advocates.

From then on, my system incorporated trying new things often. If I wasn't growing, I was standing still, and I didn't want that. Life is too short for that.

In my role, I had to conduct sales calls. For a while, I excelled at them, but eventually the players got bigger and I needed more training. I wished that my previous managers had given me better experiences to build on. And so, when I became a manager, I took my manager prospects out and gave them guided experiences. In the process, I realized that, often, they could do more than I could in a day. I refocused my efforts on training all my employees, not just manager prospects. Sales took off. My career skyrocketed, and I thought the higher-ups would be thrilled.

Fast-forward two years. I'd gotten the attention of the higher-ups, but they were far from thrilled. In fact, they asked me to stop. I wasn't doing things "the corporate way." Considering I wasn't breaking any specific guidelines, I refused. In turn, they slowly started to make my life difficult at work.

I was angry again.

I reflected on the idea that I had three choices: quit, try to change my situation, or hit the outrageous goals the higher-ups were now setting for me.

I initially determined that the best option for me was to try and hit the goals. They were difficult but possible. Through reflection, though, I realized the more significant problem: I was unwanted. My managers were trying to get me written up for the same thing three times so they could either fire me or get me to lose my bonus and quit. With that in mind, I changed my mind and decided I'd quit.

I'd just started working toward my MBA and knew that eventually, considering the workload, I'd have to quit my job anyway. I simply needed to speed up the process. I wasn't ready to quit immediately, as I'd have no source of income. I'd need to get a new job—one that wouldn't require as much mental energy.

I asked myself what I had to do. Then I planned out every month and broke that down into weeks, then days, then tasks. I focused only on the task at hand at any given moment. In taking the time to plan the long term, I was able to focus on the present.

Focusing on just the next step helped me get through it. Over time, it became apparent that I was correct in assuming my managers wanted me to leave. I was prepared. I kept an open mind and didn't fight it. I gave my notice and moved on.

I feared the unknown. What if the new job I'd gotten was terrible? The benefits and pay were also a lot less. But it ended up being the best decision for me at that time. I had to let go of my attachment to the image of myself with the big corporate job, and that was difficult, but I loved myself unconditionally and knew I was still me without that job.

Focusing on only the task at hand helped me do something I wouldn't have thought possible, so I added that to my system as well: When something seems too big, first deal with the emotions, then break down the big picture and focus on the next tiny step, one step at a time.

In the process of creating my system, I learned a lot from others as well. For example, I once had to deliver bad news about a new bonus structure to an employee I was training. They understood that this structure affected me too, and it prompted this conversation.

"Do you ever get angry?" they asked. "I've never seen you angry."

"Would it help you if I got angry?" I replied.

"I don't know. Our previous manager used to get so angry that he'd throw things."

"Did that help you reach your goals?"

"No. I was more focused on not making them angry."

I nodded. "Just because I don't show it doesn't mean I'm not angry. I am. I just don't think it's appropriate or helpful to show it at work."

Deep down, though, I was curious. Was there another way? It didn't feel good to hide my emotions.

With that in mind, I started to try new ways of addressing my emotions, including telling others about them and excusing myself so I could scream silently. The only thing that truly made me feel better, though, was to feel my feelings. In situations that didn't allow space for this, I'd set aside time to do so—as quickly as possible. Worst-case scenario, within twenty-four hours. It was odd and difficult but simple. I feared that maybe one day I'd confront a sentiment that would prove too much for me and send me spiraling out of control, but that never happened.

Sometimes I'd just need a good cry or to sleep after feeling my emotions. Sometimes I needed a physical outlet, such as exercise, hitting something (nonliving and ideally easily replaced or fixed!), or yelling. Over time, processing my emotions gave me tremendous clarity. (Remember, processing = acknowledging, accepting, and embracing the emotion until you can let it go and then learn from it.) It allowed me to see the bigger picture more often and make difficult choices. That motivated me to continue. Feeling my emotions in the moment is part of my system now too.

The more I added to my system, the more difficult it became to follow it consciously. Life comes at you fast, and it's easy to get caught up and just react if you don't have habits in place. Reflection was vital in the medium term. With reflection, I could give myself space to be aware enough to apply my system—and I could be kind to myself when I didn't apply it. In the short term this didn't work, however. In the short term, I'd react and fall back on old ways. Still, I stayed curious and kept trying new things.

The thing that ended up allowing me to stick to my system was so simple that I felt a little sheepish for not doing it earlier: I started giving myself just one minute before I did anything. I couldn't always reflect, but I could always spare a minute, and that was usually all that was needed to apply my system to the situation. I needed to pause. Pausing allowed me to quickly apply what I'd learned in previous reflections.

My system looked like this.

Stop, take a minute. If I feel something, I need to feel it. After feeling it, I can accept it or embrace it, or at the very least not let it hold me back. If other individuals are involved, I must actively listen and seek to understand them. Then, before I do what needs to be done, I must take a minute and consider the short, medium, and long term—the point of doing what I'm about to do. Because I've spent time reflecting, I know that what I do is worth doing. I must remember that if it's a little scary and challenging, I will grow, and if it seems impossible, I can focus on the next baby step. Afterwards, I'll reflect on how it went and what could have been done differently. I'll end with gratitude.

I ask myself, "What's the point of this? What do I and/or the world get out of it?" This is the short term.

Then I ask myself, "What's the big picture medium term? What do I and/or others get out of it?"

Finally, I ask myself, "How will this help me grow? What do I alone get out of it?" This is the long term.

I built my system on a foundation of reflection and gratitude, and I still use it to this day. If something comes up that I can't address in the moment, I schedule it for later. I use a calendar app and schedule everything, no matter how small. This may seem like too much structure, but this structure gives space to be present. After I schedule it, I forget about it and return to the moment; being present is a top priority. If I fail, that's in the past. I'll learn and adjust for the future, but it won't hold me back, and I won't sit idly waiting for the future either.

I know I'll continue to discover new ways to apply my system to everything I do.

Breaking it down

We all have a system–a set of guidelines and habits that directs us through life–but so often we're not conscious of it. When you become conscious of your system, you can actively improve it to help you live the life you want and become the person you want to be. These are guidelines, like being positive more than 50% of the time or being vegetarian at least 90% of the time, they fit who we are. Becoming conscious of your system will also help you determine what you love to do, which ultimately will give you purpose. The first chapter of *Dinner* is about becoming conscious of your system and starting to work with it.

Your system is unique. It must cater to *you*. Keep this in mind as you consider the various suggestions in the book. I created my system through my experiences, my goals, and the people around me. For example, take a nap everyday. You can use my experience as an example and apply the generalities to your system. Start with the suggestions that resonate with you. Then embrace who you are and, through trial and error, adjust course and continue to add and subtract elements to your system while living your life.

The bottom line is this: a good system will embrace your uniqueness.

Systems in action—working with your system

During a session with a client, she explained her day to me. Riley had woken up early, as usual, to exercise before work. She was in a high-power position and had a day full of meetings. After a difficult meeting, she took a minute before her next one and realized something was off. She excused herself and spent five minutes alone in the bathroom.

She was upset, and she acknowledged that she didn't have the space to fully feel this at the moment. So, she pulled out her phone, opened her calendar, and extended her end-of-day reflection time. Then she sent a text to her partner saying she'd be home late.

Next, she took a deep breath and told herself it was okay to be upset and that she'd deal with it at the end of the day. She took a minute to think about her next meeting. She was able to ask herself her short-, medium-, and long-term questions. What was the point of the meeting? To come out with a solution to the problem, short term. Why does it matter? It was what the team needs to be able to complete the project, medium term. How do I grow? It needs to be a solution that addresses all individuals, which is my goal long term. At this point, she was ready for her next meeting.

At the end of the day, she reflected. She wanted to think about the meeting that had upset her, but for some reason, all she could think about was her child. Instead of fighting it, she let herself go with it.

Why? she asked.

She realized she felt guilty about yelling at her child that morning. She'd said she'd play with them before leaving, but she'd ended up running late. Her toddler had thrown a fit, and Riley had yelled at them to snap out of it.

Riley allowed herself to feel the guilt. Then she let it go and resolved to apologize to and play with her child the moment she got home.

Now she could think about the meeting. She felt upset and then let the emotion go. With mental clarity, she determined she was taking something personally. She scheduled a meeting with the appropriate person to address it.

She ended her reflection session thinking about one thing she was thankful for. That day, she felt grateful to be in her position. Feeling this gratitude gave her even more courage to address the issue.

* * *

To get working on your system, reflect on your daily life. What do you do every day? How do you do these things? Look for patterns. Over time, you'll become conscious of the system you're working with.

You can't adjust everything at once. You need to be honest with yourself and focus on what you can adjust to the best of your ability right now. If you don't know where to start, I suggest starting with the physical. Pay attention to the essentials: When are you waking up? What are you eating? How are you moving your body? For a week, keep track of everything you do in a day. Write it down. Ideally, you're making time to exercise, at least three times a week, eat a relatively healthy diet, at least 90% of the time, and sleep seven to eight hours daily. Do this 90 percent of the time and your body will be solid.

I like to switch up my workout routine so I don't get bored. For example, I'll go through a certain routine for two weeks, switch it up on the third, then go back to the original for two more weeks. Then I take a week off. When it comes to my diet, I eat meat only once a week, I eat sugar only once a day, and I fast for sixteen hours a day three days per week. I do this because it aligns with my priorities, but more importantly, I do this because it works for me.

The more challenging bit is addressing what you're doing out in the world.

For example, a client, Michael, worked in the publishing business, but he longed to write. He wasn't entirely sure why. Reflecting together, we determined that he wanted to write because he felt it was what others in his industry respected most. He also wanted to write novels, specifically, for the same reason. Building his system, he started writing, and writing whatever came to mind, for five minutes every day after work until it became a habit. Through the process, he discovered he wanted to write simply because of the feeling of inner self-satisfaction it gave him. And he ended up wanting to write poetry because that's what gave him the most of that feeling. He's now extending his daily writing time regularly, to find the sweet spot, the amount of time that works for him.

This example reveals how your system really is all about you. It will help you determine what truly matters to you, and why.

During a period in my life when things weren't getting done, I learned that I needed to schedule concrete time for them. At first, I scheduled only difficult things. As I started seeing the results of this (things getting done!), I decided to start scheduling things I enjoyed as well, so I could appreciate the present more. If I wanted to read a book or play a board game, I scheduled these things. This ensured I was doing things I loved every day.

My suggestion is to schedule things in a way that ensures you'll do them. Try something and then, over time, make adjustments to make your system feel more like you.

Sometimes, you'll have to try multiple approaches. Keep learning and adapting. Remember, we're "in the painting." If we don't step back, we can't see the whole picture. This is normal. Keep trying things.

Flexibility and consistency

Growing up in the inner city as a minority kid, I struggled in many ways. For most people I knew, it was incredibly difficult to get an education, to get a good job, to save, to raise a family. It had been this way for my parents, and it seemed it would be this way for me and my children. This in itself angered me. What upset me the most, though, was that it seemed no one was brave enough to try to stop the cycle. In high school, I realized I would need to be that person. I'd need to do something different. I wanted to go to college and that meant taking an uncharted path.

The odds that you'll live the kind of life you truly want to live by doing what everyone else is doing aren't good. You need to go off the path and take calculated risks. This means different things for different individuals. Reflect on what your calculated risks are. Then take them—consistently and with room for change and growth.

Earlier I said that when I was young I wanted to find universal truths to live by. What I ended up with instead was a system of personal guidelines. My system was too rigid initially, so it would fail me. This was before I fully realized the importance of emotions. I wanted a system that simply provided a right answer. My system had no mechanism for processing emotions. It had no flexibility. Once I realized this and made the appropriate tweaks, I started getting my answers and my system became what I needed—a compass showing the general direction, not the exact way.

Change is constant, so your system needs to be adaptable.

You can start making adjustments right now. You can tackle big issues in your life right now. There is so much value in consistency over time. No matter how big the obstacle you'll make progress if you consistently chip away at it. And while you chip away, reflect and consider more strategic ways to overcome it. The more consistently you reflect, the more readily you'll be able to see the challenges coming, too. You'll have perspective, and you'll get better at seeing patterns. You also need to constantly work on your system for it to be useful.

After college, I received many job offers but not the kind I wanted—I wanted to work internationally. After applying to multiple jobs daily and not hearing back, I grew angry and frustrated. I kept trying new things. I applied to different industries and searched new websites. Nothing seemed to work. I felt as if I was continually hitting my head against a wall, just in different ways!

At that point, I'd grown lazy when it came to reflection. Finally, I knew I couldn't avoid it anymore. I sat down one day and reflected:

Am I being flexible and growing out of my comfort zone? What's the most popular international job for individuals my age? I soon saw what was standing in my way: me. I knew the answer was teaching, but I hadn't applied to any teaching positions abroad—in my mind I wasn't a teacher (the idea scared me). I was going through the motions but not truly pushing myself. I hadn't made reflection part of my system yet. It wasn't a habit. For my system to work, I needed to be aware and conscious to avoid being lazy and to push myself. Consistent refection gave me awareness and consciousness.

Ultimately, I applied for teaching and writing jobs instead of the usual ones (in finance, IT, and management) and was offered a position updating an international guidebook. The thought terrified me. Writing had always felt like my greatest weakness.

Working with your strengths and embracing your weaknesses

Though I'd learned to write in English before Spanish, I'd learned to speak Spanish years before. I more naturally thought in Spanish even when I wrote in English, which resulted in a lot of awkward writing. I feared someone would find out that I was a fraud. Writing never had and probably never would come easily to me. It took me years to accept that this was okay.

After countless hours spent trying to improve various weaknesses, I realized it wasn't worth all the time and energy. For me, it was better to spend just enough time on the weaknesses so that they didn't hold me back and instead focus the bulk of my energy on my strengths. Doing so gave me an edge. You might consider using this philosophy when tweaking your system. Think of Michael Jordan. The time he invested in basketball, his strength, made him one of the greatest players in history. The time invested in baseball—not so much.

My writing was a weakness, but it was acceptable. I'd been hired for a job. Still, accepting this job was like looking over a cliff edge before jumping into a lake and seeing no bottom. I knew I needed to be uncomfortable to grow, though. I gained awareness of this through reflection. (I was focused on attempting to make it a habit.)

I've spent years "jumping," and I still get scared. I seek out that which is scary. For me, there's great value in using fear as a guide. Whenever I lean into fear my way, it leads to growth. What "uncomfortable" emotions could you use to help you grow? How might you focus your energy on your strengths while embracing your weaknesses and the things that stretch you out of your comfort zone?

Having a custom system that embraces your uniqueness is crucial to living a purposeful life. Become conscious of your system and adjust it consistently to fit your needs. Start small and build from there.

Tips for building your system

- *First and foremost, internalize the belief that you're in control of your life. Then get to know your priorities.* They'll likely change over time, so focus on your current wants and needs. Be kind to yourself, be kind to your circle, and acknowledge that creating a system that's effective can take time.[1]
- Before you go trying to find the perfect system, *know that nothing is perfect.* Again, focus on your current wants and needs. The way is the answer. Enjoy developing and using your system today. You don't have to be afraid to fail; let curiosity lead you. As you get things wrong, your wants and needs will become clearer, and you can adjust your system as necessary.

[1] A client, Sam, established that she wanted to spend more time at home—this was a priority for her. Through various exercises, she slowly and gradually went from spending 80 percent of her time at work to 50 percent of her time there. After the first week of spending 50 percent of her time at home, she was miserable. Through reflection, she realized that she was most satisfied when she was at work about 70 percent of the time. Once she embraced this knowledge, she stopped fighting herself and changed her work hours again. She was much more satisfied as a result. Later, when she had children, she tweaked these percentages again in a way that worked for her.

- You'll need to *embrace everything about you* in order for your system to be effective. Show yourself compassion when addressing issues you've avoided dealing with. It's natural to avoid the things we dislike or struggle with. This is where the work of *Breakfast* will help. You are good enough, right now.
- It takes work to develop a system, and you'll probably put it off. We tend to spend our energy on what's urgent,[2] putting out fires in the short term. *Ground yourself in reflection.* It will help you see that putting off the long term now comes at a higher cost big picture long-term.
- *Focus on the tiniest first steps.* For example, if you want to write a book but feel overwhelmed at the magnitude of the project, start by scheduling five minutes a day to write. Don't focus on writing. Focus on making showing up a habit.
- *Reward yourself.* Schedule fun activities after difficult ones.
- *Look to others to help you.* Let them offer perspective on the big picture medium-term.
- *Remember, even the most successful people became the best through practice and hard work.* Natural talent can only take you so far. Practice and fail. Failing leads to learning and growing. It will get easier.
- *Don't judge your system.* If something works for you and feels right, do it (assuming it doesn't hurt others).
- You can do anything you choose with enough time. Once you accept this, the question becomes, *Should I do this? Trying is*

---

[2] A note about urgent versus *important*. Stop and take a "minute" to assess the situation. Sometimes we need to let the urgent fire burn so that we can realign with what's important in the long term. It's okay to let urgent fires burn if you're directing your energy to avoiding future fires and focusing on the roots of the problem. In my corporate job, there was always too much. If I attempted to do everything, I did everything poorly and burned myself out. I needed to let certain things burn and focus on the roots of the problems. For example, I kept trying to hit my sales goals (an urgent fire) and couldn't devote attention to anything else. Finally, I let my sales slip a little to give myself time to train my employees to sell. The result: no more urgent fires from sales. I set myself up for the long term.

often the only way to answer this. You'll start seeing patterns over time. You'll learn what has better odds of working for you (this involves accepting parts of yourself along the way).
- *Feel your emotions first.* When you're at peace, focus on a plan. Your system should bridge your ideal with your reality. For example, say you can't meditate because you're worried about a bill. Feel that emotion, let it go, then come up with a plan to deal with the bill as best you can. Then return to the now, to the meditation. Don't focus on what you could do tomorrow or what you could have done yesterday–focus on what you can do now, no matter how small.

Reflection and your system

No matter what your system looks like, time for reflection is critical. Even if it's just for five minutes a day. Even if it's just for one.

After reflecting, do what you think is best, for example, listen to understand. Then reflect again after you do it. Remember to feel your emotions first and then incorporate what worked into your system–asking lots of open-ended questions. Leave the rest. Next time, try the action again but change one aspect of it, no matter how small, such as trying to summarize in your own words more. Repeat. Do this with anything you deem worth doing. This is how you grow and develop your system.

While it's not helpful to dwell on the past, it can be beneficial to spend time reflecting on it, if only to be able to let it go. What patterns do you see? What lessons are you repeating? We often fall into the same holes because we never give ourselves time to reflect on a particular aspect of ourselves. Perhaps we deny that it exists. We run because we can't accept that part of us. With reflection, you can.

Reflect and accept that part of you–every part of you. Create a tool out of it. Remember, nothing is good or bad. It's about what we do with it. For example, if you're a perfectionist and feel frustrated by this, accept it and realize you've come this far in your life despite this characteristic. Once you accept this, you can use it as a tool. When is it helpful to be a perfectionist? How has it helped you get where you are? Understand it and then set guidelines to keep it in check. Make it part of your system.

Let's take the example of Jesse, a client. She was struggling with being a perfectionist. Everything had to be perfect, and meetings took forever. She wanted to connect with clients, but clients did not want her long sessions. Through reflection, she embraced her perfectionism as her medium-term goal and connecting with clients as her long-term goal. Jesse came up with a plan. She would focus on planning the agenda with a clear, agreed-upon deadline, allowing her to embrace her perfectionism before the meetings, her medium-term goal. Then she took on a more supportive role in discussions, allowing her to focus on connecting with clients as her long-term goal. The agenda addressed her short-term goal of shorter sessions. It worked.

You don't have to deconstruct an interaction or experience every time you stop and reflect, but you can acknowledge that you might benefit from reflecting on it more later. This is enough. You can't break down an issue in a minute, but you can apply your system—your tools and guidelines—in a "minute", and that's all it takes to break the cycle of the urgent. And even if you still fall into a hole, you'll be better equipped for next time.

Remember to feel your emotions first, appreciate how far you've come, and focus on what you can do now to bridge your ideal with your reality, no matter how small. Your system will evolve over time, so enjoy the process of developing and using it today. Anything you need or want to do can be done a million different ways. So often we get stuck because we think we're trying something different but we really aren't. If we keep hitting that wall in different ways, reflection can help us stop trying to go through it and instead go around or over it. Stay open.

The power of building your own system

As a coach, my job is to help individuals find long-term solutions to their challenges. After listening to understand, I could simply give people solutions that I feel would work, but I don't—because my solutions are just that. Mine. They would likely work for me but not necessarily for other people. Instead, I ask open-ended questions that guide clients toward their own solutions. What's fascinating is that in all my years of coaching, not one client has ever come up with the same solution that I would. They come up with their own, and doing so empowers them. It gives them the best odds of success.

This is why it's so important to develop a system that allows you to act in a way that suits who you are. *Breakfast* is fulfillment within yourself. *Lunch* is meaning from your circle. *Dinner* is purpose gained from what you do in the world, and at the heart of this is your uniqueness.

For example, imagine you're buying dog food. In the store, you'll find numerous options, perhaps to the point where it's overwhelming. Now imagine your dog has no teeth. Suddenly, there are significantly fewer options. You need food specifically for dogs with no teeth. This "weird" trait is now helpful. Your unique characteristics aren't good or bad: they're information you can use to help you choose how you spend your time.

The key to developing a system that works for you is to take consistent action. Try new things, learn, and be flexible. Try things that speak to you first—if you don't believe something will help you, it won't. And I don't recommend trying several things at once; start with one or two at a time to help you stay focused and avoid getting overwhelmed. Decide how long you'll try them, and when that time is up, assess how they're going. Continue with what works and try something new regarding what isn't working. Find your "just right."

Over time, you'll create a system of guidance that's unique to and best for you and only you. This will lead to habits. This system will allow you to embrace your why and your how (which we'll explore shortly). It's worth the work.

A reflection session

It's Friday night. I'm doing my weekly reflection, and I'm annoyed. I didn't get to the important things–there was always something more urgent. I feel like a loser. This isn't the first week I've spent ignoring the important and focusing on the urgent.

Why? I ask myself.

I can't reflect yet. I need to feel it.

I let myself sulk for a few minutes, and the feeling slowly fades. The pity party is over.

I let myself down.

Why?

I had a list of things I needed to get done, but I spent my time putting out urgent fires. I did a lot daily, just not what I wanted to do.

Why?

I have no idea.

Did I need to say 'no' more? I attempted this last month. Do I need to invest more effort into saying no or look at this from a different angle? What's worked in the past? I need to try something new.

I give myself five minutes. After five minutes, all I've come up with is "schedule it all."

I'll schedule it all. Everything will be given a time slot and I'll follow the schedule to the letter–the hard, the easy, the fun, and the ugly. This should help me say no. A yes requires a time slot.

After writing the schedule, I look it over. Something seems off. I compare it to my previous week. It doesn't seem realistic.

That's the issue. I need to give up the urgent things now and not even schedule them. This will give me time to prepare for the important.

I feel better. I have a plan. I don't know if it will work, but I think I can let myself enjoy the weekend now.

Takeaways

- Don't try to create the perfect system. Instead, focus on your current wants and needs and find inner self-satisfaction in developing and using your system today. And remember that your system should encompass everything about you, even the aspects of yourself you struggle with.
- Try not to get too attached to any one aspect of your system. Be curious and flexible. Remember that failure leads to learning and growing. Keep tweaking.
- Ground yourself in reflection to avoid getting stuck putting out fires. Assess the situation and let the urgent fire burn as safely as possible while directing your energy to preventing future fires.
- Stop, take a "minute", and reflect before saying or doing.
- Don't judge your system. If something feels right for you, do it (assuming it doesn't hurt others).

Questions for reflection

- What, what, what? (When in doubt, ask what.)
- What do I want?
- What do I need?
- What has worked for me in the past?

* * *

CHAPTER EIGHT

EXPLORE YOUR PASSIONS

Live your life consciously and you'll appreciate the now constantly.

Focus: A passion is something you love to do. It's generally something that feels "bigger" than you, something that gives you a sense of empowerment and helps you grow. By consciously exploring what you love to do, you'll uncover your why and your how. In this chapter, we'll look at how to connect the dots between what you love, your why, and your how—all to gain clarity on your passions. We'll explore how to use your passions to gain purpose.

Story

I had almost a dozen jobs, internships, and externships in high school and over a dozen more in college. Why? I wanted to find something I woke up excited about every morning. I believed that was what I needed to feel driven. However, it was an extremely frustrating process. I'd always be excited initially, but this feeling would fade over time, leaving me feeling unsatisfied. I eventually learned that excitement is to purpose what infatuation is to love. It's a beautiful thing, but it doesn't last.

Growing up in my world, success meant becoming a doctor or lawyer. I liked the idea of helping people in need, so becoming a doctor made the most sense to me. At fourteen, I told myself I'd become a doctor. But after shadowing doctors, I realized that this wasn't the life for me. Doctors were always on call. One that I followed missed their child's birthday due to an emergency. This didn't sit well with me. I knew then that I wanted a job that would allow me to be there for my family.

When I was young, I was fascinated by Greek mythology; the story of Achilles really spoke to me. He had to choose between a long life remembered by his family or a short one remembered by the world. I instinctively chose a long life when I read it. It was the first time I realized that family was more important to me than glory.

With reflection, I realized that *why* I wanted to become a doctor initially was the relevant part. I wanted to help people (the why), but there were many ways I could achieve this (the how). Understanding this gave me direction.

When I was sixteen, I landed an internship with my local congressional representative. I now wanted to be a politician. I was going to be a public servant and help others. I wouldn't have to choose between life and family. Thank goodness for internships, because once again I ran into a problem. Most of the politician's time was spent fundraising. I'd thought that politicians were supposed to advocate for what the majority of their constituents wanted, but what I saw seemed to be politicians doing what the majority of their constituents with money wanted.

I no longer wanted to be a politician. I was lost again. I needed to think outside the box.

I took a lengthy and expensive test that told me I should be a sports agent or a funeral director. I investigated both options, and they made sense—both would allow me to help others and enjoy a work-life balance. But they also lacked certain things I'd discovered I wanted along the way. Being a sports agent wouldn't give me a sense of being part of something bigger than me. (Being a part of something bigger is something we all need and it usually involves helping others or the world.) I wanted to feel as if I were making a difference in the world, and although I was sure agents made a big difference to those they served, it wasn't enough for me. The issue with becoming a funeral director was how I dealt with others' pain. I'm empathetic. I was good at helping others because I understood them, but I often felt their pain as my own. The thought of feeling the pain of people who had lost someone, every day, seemed exhausting.

As time went by, I started spending less time in each job I took, able to figure out more quickly that it wasn't a good fit. I started to wonder, though–would nothing be perfect? Would I have to readjust my priorities and compromise? Ultimately, a minor portion of the expensive test led me to my answer. The test results revealed that efficiency and effectiveness were two qualities I valued highly. So where did they fit into all this? It turned out they were part of my how.

After thinking long and hard about what industry helped people, I ended up in a nonprofit. In addition to teaching immigrant children English as a second language, I also worked with children with disabilities as a tutor and a soccer coach.

I immensely enjoyed my time doing these things, and this further reinforced my goal of working in a job where I could make a difference. The issue was money. For a while, I worked in publicity, where the one who paid the most decided who got a voice. In the nonprofit world, it was similar. It was great if you believed in what the donor believed, but if you thought the money could be put to a better use, too bad.

After all, money is necessary. It goes hand-in-hand with power. So what could I do that would make me money and check all the other boxes? When I couldn't find anything, I hatched an idea: I'd make a lot of money and then start my own nonprofit. I'd get to choose how to help people. In the meantime, what was the most exciting and most lucrative job I could get?

Investment banking!

And so, during college I took an internship at an investment bank. The culture wasn't a fit, but I liked the work and thought I could endure it for a few years. It was a means to an end. In addition, it solved my need for excitement–it was a challenge.

Meanwhile, I asked anyone and everyone who'd listen if they knew of people who were doing something similar to what I wanted to do. I was led to others with comparable plans, but unfortunately, the more of these people I met, the more disappointed I became. These were good people with good intentions, but the pattern was hard to deny: the longer people worked in banking the less connected they became to their plan. This industry demanded all their energy, so even if they were just in it for the money, over time, it was easy to lose sight of the big picture long term.

I didn't know if I was strong enough to overcome this obvious difficulty, and I didn't want to take the chance. I was sure people had succeeded but I didn't like the odds I was seeing. No one I'd talked to had made the switch, and these people were smarter and more motivated than I was. In the end, I decided not to pursue a career in investment banking.

Someone told me the best jobs were those you were passionate about because they never seemed like work. In college, I received lots of magazines (thanks to a magazine subscription I'd been gifted) and found myself gravitating to the cooking ones. Everything looked delicious. One day, I got up the courage to try out a dish. The momentum built from there. I tried dish after dish, kept pushing my limits, learning and growing. Eventually, I came up with the idea of opening a restaurant. I convinced my college to allow me to start one on campus; I ran it for just one night a week. Just as quickly as I'd found my passion for cooking, I lost my enthusiasm to do it for work. For me, cooking as a job took away the joy of cooking. It was frustrating to learn that sometimes passions and jobs don't mix well, but I discovered something else in the process: the thrill of running a business.

In reflection sessions, I realized that I was good at turning a profit in my endeavors. It had just never occurred to me to open my own business. I'd never been taught that this was an option. In working for myself, I saw that I was good at sales, and I was able to be effective and efficient. I was also able to invoke change when necessary.

When I eventually sought a new job, I had a new perspective. I was focused on the big picture medium term. Reflecting, I'd concluded that I needed to create a life while searching for work simultaneously. If not, life would pass me by while I tried to find the perfect job to fit the life I didn't have.

At the age of twenty-one, I found a job in sales. In this role, I had lots of freedom. I ran multiple offices how I saw fit—it was like running my own business. However, I set boundaries to prioritize balance in my life. Instead of focusing on whether this was the perfect job, I focused on how I could do my best.

After a few years, I was spending most of my time hiring and training new employees. The training was always better when I could cater it to the individual. The more I learned about the person (listening to understand), the better I could teach them. I realized then what had been staring me in the face all along: I was passionate about teaching others to be effective and efficient. It was a strength, and people were willing to pay me for it. I could do it with a focus on helping people grow (my why) in a way that was effective and efficient (my how).

I soon realized that the corporate setting wasn't ideal. I reached a point where I had too many eyes on me because I wasn't doing things by the book. I'd found the job for me, but I needed a different environment.

Breaking it down

With lots of trial and error throughout my career journey, I learned two things critical to this part of *Dinner*. First, I needed a sense of purpose, not excitement. I figured this out the hard way, but hopefully you can take something away from my journey. External feelings are fleeting. Purpose comes from within and is lasting.

Second, I needed to understand and accept my why and my how. Together, your why, your how, and what you love to do combine into your passion. Passion gives you purpose. Discovering this is a journey. For the short term, seek to feel empowered in what you do. For the medium term, ensure that what you do feels "bigger" than you. For the long term, strive to feel as if you can grow in what you do. This will keep you fueled on your journey.

Figuring out your why and your how

Understanding and accepting your 'why' and 'how' takes time and effort. It often requires reflecting on your past to find patterns—when we're young, we subconsciously strive toward our why. As we age, we tend to lose sight of it and let the world and its noise obscure it. Reflect consistently and keep trying new things to reveal the 'why' you might have lost sight of.

Why do you do the things you do? Whatever the answer, seek it out. Be open and be curious. Throughout your day, ask yourself, "Why am I doing this? What's the point? How does it fit the big picture, long term, in my life?"

Your why is what drives you, whether you're aware of it or not.

Another way to seek out your why is to first seek out your wants. For example, say you want a million dollars. Set goals and timelines around this, ensuring you incorporate time to reflect as you progress toward the goal. Once you reach $500,000, for example, stop and take inventory. Has the money given you some sense of purpose? If yes, great, continue. If no, ask yourself if more would give you purpose and why. If your answer rings true for you, pursue it further. Do this again at another milestone. *Always ask why*. If you reach your goal and believe you can gain more from going further, do that. If you realize that money won't give you purpose, ask yourself what you think will. Rinse and repeat. Over time, you'll see patterns. Each time you reach a milestone and reflect, consider the short term, the medium term, and the long term.

In my case, seeking money was a means to my why—helping others. Money in itself wouldn't give me purpose. You may, like me, need to go through a process to accept your why. Once you accept it, you can embrace it and gain purpose. Hopefully, it won't take you the decades that it took me! Hopefully you can get to your purpose more effectively and efficiently.

Try not to judge your why or fight with yourself about it. Instead, seek to understand it; this will lead to acceptance. Once you know your why, your how will become clearer.

Your how is just as important, but it's often harder to figure out because it's centered in the present rather than the past. When you're focused on your how, you're taking part in your passion simply for the sake of it. You're satisfied in the moment. There are no shortcuts to figuring out your how. You'll need to spend time reflecting and experimenting. Keep asking yourself questions.

The critical question for me was "How do I like to help people?" The answer was "Efficiently and effectively, while feeling part of something bigger and living a balanced life."

Reflect consistently, ask yourself open-ended questions, and keep trying new things. You'll figure out your why and how, and when you do, and you accept these things, you can apply them to what you love and find your passions. Often, it won't seem like "work". More importantly, doing it will give you inner self-satisfaction. This doesn't mean it won't be hard or that you won't fail. It means that you'll be satisfied in the moment and have the strength to get back up because what you're doing is right for you.

Be kind to yourself, be kind to your circle. Be curious, be consistent. Fail, learn, grow. And remember the point of it all—the now. Your how and inner self-satisfaction helps you do this.

Living along the way

It can take a long time to figure out your how and why. Meanwhile, life keeps going. Keep figuring out what you need and incorporate it into your system as you gain purpose. The patterns will become easier to see, understand, and accept with reflection. In truth, we don't get to choose our why or how—we can only strive to live them.

Don't dwell on the time it takes you to do this. Break it down, one step at a time. It will take exactly the time you need, whether that's years, decades, or longer. It doesn't matter. Life is about the journey. You can live in the moment, right now, while moving toward your purpose. In the end, *fulfillment*, *meaning*, and *purpose* are simply different ways of being present. You are enough now. You can start today. That's the secret to life.

You are good enough to start now.

Along the way, you'll learn many things about yourself. Take time to reflect on these things and accept them, one at a time (it's much easier to do this than to try to accept everything at once). Ask yourself the difficult questions. And periodically stop and appreciate the progress you're making—this will allow you to feel satisfied throughout your journey. Our current moment can be one of fulfillment, meaning, and purpose.

The most important thing is to start now.

Keep figuring out what you need to incorporate into your system to grow it. Strive to understand, accept, and embrace your why and your how. Remember, this is where purpose comes from. When you have purpose, you're satisfied in what you're doing.

A reflection session

Doing my end-of-day reflection, I realize I feel a little lost. Because of the pandemic, I can't do what I usually do for work. I need to find something new that I'm passionate about and that allows me to embrace my why and my how.

Right now, I don't have much time. I take five minutes and write down all the new things I can think of. I come up with an extensive list, but going through it, I see lots of overlap, many things I've already attempted, and many things I can't do without additional schooling. I don't want more schooling unless necessary.

What's left?

Write a book!.

I'm not a writer. Far from it. It's a weakness. It doesn't require schooling, but it does require improvement. The only way to improve is with practice. Practice means writing.

I'm scared out of my mind about it. I try to find reasons not to do it.

People don't care about what I have to say.

But there's only one way to find out if this is true.

I'm going to write a book.

Where and how will I start?

I need to do some research and break it down step-by-step.

It feels as if I'm planning to go to the moon.

I'm not going to think about that. I'll focus on breaking it down and then just take the next step.

I feel better now. (This is how I decided to write this book.)

Takeaways

- Your 'why' is the driving force that pushes you forward in life. Look to patterns in the past.
- Your 'how' fuels you in the moment.
- Uncovering and accepting your why and your how takes time and effort. Start now.
- Your passion is where your why and your how converge. Passion gives you purpose.
- When you have purpose, you're satisfied in what you're doing at the moment. It allows you to be present.

Questions for reflection

- Why am I doing this?
- How do I prefer to do this?
- What do I love to do?
- When have I failed but still felt like a winner?

* * *

CHAPTER NINE

EMBRACE YOUR PURPOSE

Do what you love and catch purpose in your glove.

Focus: To embrace your passions and to do it for the sake of doing, without getting attached to specific outcomes. The destination doesn't matter–it's all about the process. In this chapter, we'll talk about learning to find inner self-satisfaction in what you do and living your life in the moment with purpose.

Story

I was sitting outside the office, heartbroken. It wasn't a partner who'd rejected me, but the corporate job I'd fallen in love with. The sick feeling in my stomach felt familiar.

As mentioned in a previous story, I'd started focusing my energy on training my employees, catering to them as individuals. I was doing what I loved and getting great results. The problem was that my employer didn't like how I was getting them. I'd already determined that I wanted to start a business training people and had planned to leave. I just had to commence that journey earlier than anticipated.

This wasn't the first time I'd felt let down by a job. I reflected and realized I'd been seeking purpose externally, from my jobs, which was why they always let me down. Purpose comes from within. I knew I wanted to help people, and I'd accepted this, but I hadn't embraced this. Now I had no choice.

The situation brought back memories of when I hired a teacher. It had been an employer's market at the time, and James was overqualified, but he was enthusiastic. I catered my training to his needs, as I always did, and he excelled. On our way to make a delivery one afternoon, I finally asked him something that I'd been wondering about since hiring him.

"Why do you want to work here?"

"I want to work anywhere," James replied, with refreshing honesty. "I lost my job due to cutbacks."

"Why didn't you apply for another teaching job?"

"I did, many times, for months. There are no teaching jobs. I got desperate and started to apply for any good-paying job I could find."

"Was this the best offer you got?"

"This was the only offer I got. No one wants to hire a teacher to do something other than teach." He paused and looked at me. "So why did you hire me?"

"I've been doing this awhile. Assuming someone meets the basic qualifications, I look for motivation and a willingness to work hard. You had both qualities. So what's the ideal for you in five years, career-wise?"

"Ideally teaching, but who knows now? I might need help moving from sales back to teaching once the economy improves."

I nodded. "I can help you there. When I need to train the staff on something, I'm going to teach you instead, and then you'll train everyone at this office. You'll be my unofficial on-site trainer. Feel free to add that to your résumé."

James laughed. "That may be helpful one day."

"It will be today. Are you not still applying for teaching jobs?"

"No, I like this job. Why would I apply for a different job?"

"You should still be applying for other jobs. I encourage all my employees to do so. Worst case, you'll at least have a sense of choice–knowing that you don't have to work here; you choose to work here. Best case, you get back to teaching. What do you have to lose?"

"Well, applying for jobs takes time and energy."

"Break it down and take one step at a time. Apply to at least one job a month. That's doable, right?"

James nodded. "One a month, yeah. I can do that."

"In the meantime, the best investment you can make right now is in yourself. No matter where you work, you can take that with you. You'll become more valuable."

A few months later, James pulled me aside at work to talk.

"I got a teaching job, but if you ask me to stay, I will."

"This is what you wanted, no?"

"Yes, I love to teach."

"Then I'll fire you if you don't take it," I said with a smile.

"Thank you."

"You did it all yourself."

I'd been needing to have a similar conversation with myself for months. I needed to embrace my purpose. In a way, getting pushed out was a blessing. Now, I had to make a plan, break it down, and focus on the next step. Baby steps.

I received my MBA in the U.K. and soon after, I fell in love again, this time with my business. I started creating training programs focused on the individual. However, though lots of people expressed support, only one gave me business. This was disheartening. I'd done everything "right," and it wasn't working out.

Several months later, a friend highlighted that I needed something to make me stand out in the field. "What else do you like?" they asked. "What else are you good at?"

Besides sales and training, not much, I thought. *I cook, I dance, and I play board games.*

"Just pick something and use it to stand out."

Willing to give it a try, as per my system, I created custom board games to accompany my training—and it worked. People became more willing to try my services. Working with that idea and tweaking it, I decided to market my business as bespoke training centered around board games. I did okay with this, but it proved tricky because my partner and I were moving every few years.

One year and countless meetings with companies later, it was clear I needed a portfolio of premade trainings instead, at least in the country I was in. This was another blow to the heart, but I got to work. Things started to move. I got more callbacks. I learned many lessons along the way and was grateful for any opportunity. I'd finally figured it out—and then we moved to a different country, a Spanish-speaking country, where everyone wanted to have training in Spanish. I should have been grateful that I knew and could train in Spanish. Instead, I felt betrayed. The goalpost kept moving.

I took a few months and recreated my training in Spanish, but before establishing myself, we moved again, this time to Asia. Another blow to the gut. I felt like Sisyphus rolling that boulder uphill only to have it roll back down every time. I was determined and ready to do whatever it took, however.

During this time, our first child was born. For the first five weeks, they were in the ICU. When we were able to take them home, it was clear that one of us would need to care for our baby 24/7. They had a monitor and needed constant supervision—as in, someone had to be within arm's distance to shake them if their heart stopped. My partner couldn't stay home. She'd tried in the past and couldn't deal with not having work. Plus, though I made more money, she had a far more secure position. I accepted this and stepped up, though I didn't stop my work entirely. I merely slowed down and underwent an internal metamorphosis.

I couldn't do company training, but I could offer coaching to individuals. I created a guide. I had found a way. Then the pandemic hit. Down for the count again. Online was no substitute for in-person coaching. It was more difficult and less effective for both the client and me. (It took a large amount of time and energy to eventually become effective.) No matter what, I was doomed to fail, it seemed. Still, I wouldn't stop. I determined I needed to do the unimaginable: write a book. This guide.

Around this time, I realized something extraordinary that changed everything for me: I'd been doing what I loved and living my why all along. I'd been doing it but not enjoying the fruits of my labor. I'd been focusing on specific outcomes, not the journey, which I'd been blind to. All along the way, I'd been teaching people and helping them grow. I simply had to let go of my attachment to a specific idea of what this looked like.

Once I accepted this, I felt a sense of purpose. I appreciated the moment. I embraced my why and my how in everything—actively.

I would write the book because I could see the purpose in it. I would write it to help others. It wouldn't matter if the book failed because the next thing would incorporate my why and my how. I had purpose now, and I would continue to have purpose.

The biggest revelation was around purpose with my child. My purpose is to help people. In choosing to stay home and raise my child, I unconsciously chose to help them.

I teach my child to stop and reflect for a "minute" (break down at the end of this guide) before doing or saying anything. I teach them how to address their emotions. I teach them to do what's right for them, assuming they're not hurting others. I teach them to love themselves. I teach them all this through my example. (There is no room for fear, only love.) This is the biggest accomplishment of my life, and now I fully embrace every moment of it. I love the challenge of doing it efficiently and effectively and accepting my child as the unique individual they are. I might fail, my child might not appreciate it, and others might not understand it, but I don't care about any of that because it gives me purpose. It rings true to me. Doing what I love is what I'm meant to do, and the act of doing it in the moment is all I need.

What comes next? Who knows!

Breaking it down

Embracing what you're doing in the moment is a powerful way to gain a sense of purpose. You might already be doing what you love but forgetting to feel the purpose that comes with it because you're too focused on outcomes. By letting go and embracing your passions, you can find purpose within, allowing you to be present in the moment.

You can do it. Use your system to embrace what you love to do now. Let go and be present.

Releasing attachment

Dinner is about doing what you love in the world. It's about embracing your purpose. Before you can do this, though, you have to release attachment to a particular idea of what your purpose looks like.

For example, let's say your passion is playing football. Being part of a team gives you inner self-satisfaction (your why), and you enjoy practicing and approaching the game systematically (your how). Along the way, though, you get attached to the idea of playing professionally. So you strive for it and get disappointed when it doesn't happen, forgetting about the purpose that playing football gives you.

You don't have to get stuck on this goal. You can still choose to keep trying to play professionally, *and* you can embrace your purpose now. What does this look like? Maybe you accept that offer to play in the third-tier league, or find a coaching job.

When you stop attaching yourself to a particular idea around your purpose, you can more easily see the many opportunities in your life. Plan for the future, seek out your dreams, *and* enjoy what you're doing now. It is important to set a deadline. Set a time to assess whether you need to pivot or give yourself more time. Do you need to change your plan or goal? It is critical to be honest with yourself throughout this whole process.

An analogy that works for me is to think of life as a video game. Starting a new level is fun. Then comes the struggle. It feels good to advance and get new tools, but as I do, the levels get more complex. Just when I feel I've figured out one level of my life, I go to the next one and another difficulty comes into view. It never ends—so I can choose to hold my breath until it gets easy, or I can enjoy the game now. I can reflect and appreciate my purpose in the moment.

Again, life isn't about where you're going but how you get there. You can be fulfilled in loving yourself; you can create meaning by loving the people in your circle; and you can experience purpose in doing what you love.

This can all happen in the here and now.

Getting comfortable with your how

There's purpose to be found in everything you do. The world can make it difficult to do what you love, but this is where embracing your how comes in. You might not always be able to do what you love, but you can always live with your how in mind. Simultaneously, you can seek out different circumstances to eventually do what you love. Try now. You are enough now.

It took a few years of attempting to do what I loved while holding onto expectations and caring about what others thought before I realized that I had to let that all go. My how was the first step to letting go of the specifics. This led me to my passion and allowed me to enjoy the journey. It was the result of reflecting, trying, and failing. I now have purpose in the moment. I don't care if others appreciate it or if things change. That's all there is to it. It's simple–and it takes an enormous amount of work.

Your how gives you short-term energy, while your why gives you medium-term direction, and your passion gives you long-term purpose. Ideally, you're balancing all three. Before doing anything that isn't already part of your system, stop and ask yourself, "What's the point, short term? How does it fit the big picture, medium term? How does it give me purpose (or fulfillment or meaning) long term?"

It's okay if you're not making a living doing what you love right now. You can still live with your how at the forefront and seek out your why and your passions. Focus on the aspects of what you're doing right now that connect to your how. It starts with appreciating the small things every day. Take the next tiniest step and consistently try something new to get you closer to doing what you love. You can always find ways to energize yourself in the moment.

Tips for living in the now while seeking your purpose

- Refrain from getting caught up in the past. You are where you are now. The best way to move forward is to accept this.
- Similarly, refrain from waiting for the future. You are enough now. Try now.
- Every month, choose something you like about yourself and say it aloud every morning. And/or, before interacting with others, choose two words you want to exemplify and repeat them to yourself on a loop for a minute beforehand.
- Be prepared for the worst case and plan for your ideal.
- Keep reflecting, planning, and trying things if you're not content with what you're doing. It's okay not to love your job, as you can still focus on how to energize yourself, but it's not okay to stay in a job that you are miserable in. You might need it to make a living, but you don't need to stay there indefinitely. Make a plan to leave.
- Be open and aim not to judge opportunities before trying them. If something works for you, that's all that matters. It's not about being one-hundred-percent certain. Take calculated risks that are right for you.

The power of purpose (Be like water)

When you have a sense of purpose, it's easier not to care about outcomes as much. It's easier to be successful in a way that's not attached to a title or a position or what the world thinks of you. If you let it all go, you can be full now. Change and failure might still be painful, but no matter what, that sense of purpose will remain.

There isn't much that sticks to ice (except maybe your tongue!). Things tend to slide right off it. Be like ice externally in what you do. Sometimes we need to be like steam externally and let things go through us, let go, and not take it personally. Sometimes we need to be like liquid and adapt to our circumstances or others. Other times, we need to be like ice and not get attached to specific outcomes.

Focus on the how. It will allow you to appreciate the moment. And focus on the why. It will offer a direction. You are who you are. Accept and embrace that. You can move through the world with purpose right now, just the way you are.

A reflection session

I'm doing my monthly reflection. (I do daily, weekly, monthly, and annual reflections.) I've experienced many failures this month, but I'm focusing on reflecting on them, learning from them, and trying new things—this last part is the most crucial. I might not try anything new today, but I'll schedule time to do so.

My book is going at a glacial pace. What can I do to improve this process?

I've given myself deadlines, and despite consistently hitting them, I'm failing in the big picture medium term. Every next step breaks down to three or four, it seems. I've attempted many things that have only marginally helped.

What should I do? What does my system say about situations like this?

I'm good with myself and feel fulfilled. I'm good in my circle; I have meaning. I'm feeling a sense of purpose in what I'm doing. What am I missing?

When you struggle, ask for help.

That makes sense. I need to ask for help.

What new thing could I try? How could someone help me?

I reflect and realize that my windows to write have been quite short. I work better with longer windows. I need help creating longer windows and more opportunities to write.

I'll reach out to my partner during our weekly check-in (which is like reflection with another person) *and ask for her help. I'm not sure how exactly she'll be able to, but I trust we can figure it out together. Maybe she'll be able to pick up some extra duties around the house for a couple of weeks. In asking her, I'll be allowing my circle to support me in the medium term. And ultimately, writing this book is giving me purpose in the long term.*

That feels right. I plan for this. I let go. I can now go back to being present.

Takeaways

- Release attachment to a particular idea of what living your purpose looks like and be open to your passions now.
- Your how gives you energy in the short term; it keeps you going.
- Your why gives you direction in the medium term; it pushes you.
- Your passion gives you purpose in the long term while allowing you to be satisfied with what you're doing right now.

Questions for reflection

- What's the short-term goal of this? What's the point?
- What's the medium-term goal of this? How does it fit the big picture medium term?
- What's the long-term goal? What do I get out of it?
- What do I feel satisfied doing just for the sake of doing it (regardless of the outcome)?

* * *

DINNER

FINAL THOUGHTS

Learn to not attach and you'll be unmatched.

Ideally, work on *Breakfast, Lunch and Dinner* all at the same time. The main ingredient in *Dinner* is your system. Focus on doing what works for you. Figure out what this is by consistently trying new things, however small. Create habits out of what works.

Two other important ingredients are your why and your how. Where they meet with what you love to do, you'll find your passions. And your passions will give you purpose. Purpose comes from within. Purpose gives you inner self-satisfaction. It allows you to let go of outcomes and be present now. That's the true goal. Presence.

In summary, here's what we explored in Chapters Seven, Eight, and Nine:

- Your system is what works for you. Don't judge it.
- Learn, adapt, and appreciate the journey.
- Use reflection to become conscious of what you're doing right now.
- The past can help us figure out our patterns and our why, but we don't have to let it hold us back.
- We can plan for the future, but we don't have to wait to take action. Start now. Life is now.
- In all things, consider the short term, medium term, and long term.

When it comes to living a life of fulfillment, meaning, and purpose, the most important thing to remember is to be present. Then, let curiosity be your guide. Stop judging and start doing what works for you. Your life is happening right now, be present.

SOME DESSERT TO SATISFY

I learned long ago to take power away from a bully by agreeing with them. If the world says that putting yourself first is selfish, be like steam externally and let these words go through you. "Yes, I am selfish, and that's okay. I want to help others, and I must take care of myself first."

In a world that often criticizes selfishness, it can be difficult to prioritize your needs. Just remember that by putting yourself first, you can better help others. Ultimately, we need to be selfish with our needs internally to be selfless with others and the world. This gives us what we need externally from others and the world.

I'll say it again for the people in the back: you are good enough now. Learn to live in the present and enjoy the moment the way you want to enjoy it. Over the years, my life improved because I improved my mindset. Anyone can do this.

You can do this.

Hopefully this guide has pointed you in the right direction and given you some tools to get started, but it's up to you to invest the time and create a system that works for you–that's unique to you. Only you can create fulfillment, meaning, and purpose in your life, so don't be afraid to be selfish and start living the life you want to live, one moment at a time.

- When you have fulfillment, you feel you belong in yourself. This is Breakfast.
- When you have meaning, you feel you belong with others. This is Lunch.
- When you have purpose, you feel you belong in the world. This is Dinner.

The dessert is love.
Love yourself, love others, and love what you do.

Along the way, try not to judge yourself, others, or the world. Seek to be open and curious. Avoid getting attached to specific outcomes or qualities in yourself or others. Life is the journey. Everything and everyone will change over time, and that's normal! All we have is now–learn to appreciate this and you will always be satiated. It's pleasant to remember eating ice cream, and it's fun to look forward to eating it, but nothing beats actually eating it, right now. You can't taste the past or the future.

If you take away just one tool from this guide, take reflection

Reflection is the most significant concept in this guide. It will help you digest Breakfast, Lunch, and Dinner. At its heart, reflection is simply time to process life–time to become conscious of where you came from, where you are, and where you're going. Like everything, the only way to get good at it is through practice. It's likely that the more you reflect, the more you'll want to reflect. Don't limit yourself. Do as much as you need.

When in doubt, be like a toddler and ask why, how, or what.

If you hit something big and scary during reflection, break it down. Make a plan and start with the smallest of steps. Believe in yourself and keep at it. Give yourself time. Slow and steady.

If you find yourself struggling with consistency (as most of us do), try rewarding yourself for reflecting. Or do it for just two minutes a day. Whatever you need to make it a habit. Just show up. Ultimately, it doesn't matter how long it takes you to reach your goals. Each of us has the ability to determine the answers to our problems. What we need is the time and space to listen to ourselves.

Remember, in those high-pressure, no-time-to-stop moments, the best thing to do is pause. "What's the point?" (short term). "How does this fit the bigger picture?" (medium term). "How does this help me?" (long term). Then, even if you fail, you can fall back on the knowledge that you did your best—you did what was right for you.

Doing your best, for you

No matter how much of this kind of work you do, you'll sometimes struggle to appreciate the moment. This is normal. You're human, and it's easy to get caught up in the noise. All you can do is your best in the moment, your version of "smelling the roses." Try to focus on balance. When planning, remember to schedule fun.

Sometimes you need to let the urgent fire burn—and maybe the fire needs to consume everything so you can start anew. Understanding why it started might just be more important than putting it out so you can prevent similar fires in the future.

Lean on your love for yourself. And when it all feels like too much, lean on your circle. Ask for help when you need help. That's what your circle is there for. Help only arrives if you let it. You can also lean on your system. Together, these things allow you to live in the present.

If all else fails, look to death. It's going to happen whether you like it or not. Reflecting on it will look different and result in different actions for everyone. It might mean you end up distancing yourself from someone you love (that doesn't mean you stop loving them; it just means they can't hurt you anymore). It might mean accepting that part of yourself you've always scorned. It might mean taking a leap of faith and trying something new. If doing X gives you purpose, do it. Who cares what anyone else thinks? What if you die tomorrow? The best moment of your life is now. Get the most out of it.

I hope you can see the concepts in this book as a bridge from where you are now to your fulfillment, meaning, and purpose. The world won't give you these things. You give them to yourself. Take that first step—the hardest one—and continue moving. The goal is to be present.

Pick an idea that resonates with you and just try it. Give yourself a time limit, then reflect on what worked and incorporate it; leave the rest. Next, try another idea. It's okay to fail. Pause to reflect along the way, adjust course as necessary, and appreciate the growth.

Your path is different from mine, but our guiding truths are the same: we need to love ourselves, we need the love of others, and we need to do things we love. It's all about love. It's the simplest path to living in the moment.

You are enough now.

Start now.

TAKE A "MINUTE"

Be Conscious.

1. Stop and Breathe.
(Deeply in, hold, slowly let it out. Repeat if necessary.)
2. Process your emotions.
(Label, feel, let go.)

Be Curious

3. Ask questions.
(Ask yourself why, ask others wow, be a detective.)
4. Gain perspective.
(What is the point? What is the big picture?)

Be Open

5. Try your way.
(Listen, communicate, or do it now. You are enough.)
6. Be present.
(Gain satisfaction from the act of trying.)

**Bonus for after: learn, let go and appreciate.*

Thank you for reading my guide.

If you enjoyed yourself, please consider leaving a review.

More importantly, if you know someone who might benefit from this guide, please recommend the book.

www.ingramcontent.com/pod-product-compliance
Lightning Source LLC
LaVergne TN
LVHW010918110826
845149LV00013B/2413